A Strawberry Moon Above Kibbutz Gvulot

A remarkable family history, spanning more than a hundred years

by

Lena Glinoer

Grosvenor House
Publishing Limited

All rights reserved
Copyright © Lena Glinoer, 2024

The right of Lena Glinoer to be identified as the author of this work has been asserted in accordance with Section 78 of the Copyright, Designs and Patents Act 1988

The book cover is copyright to Lena Glinoer

This book is published by
Grosvenor House Publishing Ltd
Link House
140 The Broadway, Tolworth, Surrey, KT6 7HT.
www.grosvenorhousepublishing.co.uk

This book is sold subject to the conditions that it shall not, by way of trade or otherwise, be lent, resold, hired out or otherwise circulated without the author's or publisher's prior consent in any form of binding or cover other than that in which it is published and without a similar condition including this condition being imposed on the subsequent purchaser.

A CIP record for this book
is available from the British Library

ISBN 978-1-80381-696-8

In memory of…

My parents, Lydia and Guydon Glinoer

My maternal grandmother, Edwarda Szklarzowna
&
Those who risked everything to save the lives of others

About the Author

Lena Glinoer was born in Paris in 1965. She has always been fascinated by her Jewish ancestry and was fortunate enough to have been told many stories over the years by close family members which she began noting down and recording from a young age. The author lives in London with her husband and daughter and a very handsome marmalade cat.

Preface

Over a period of time from the 1980's to 1990's, I had the good sense to record on audio tape and write down some of the experiences my parents had lived through during their childhoods and early life. I also had many conversations with my maternal grandmother, who left a memoir describing some of the major events in her life. If it were not for that combination of fascination (on my part) and generosity (on their part) this work would never have come to be. Somehow, I wanted to preserve and weave something whole and complete from all the precious fragments given to me by people whose stories and experiences mattered deeply. I promised myself that, one day, I would write all about it.

Some thirty years or more have now passed since I started noting down these extraordinary accounts. And after many attempts, here is the finished work, inspired by the people who were always kind and patient enough to share many wonderful and personal anecdotes with me which I have sewn together, piece by piece. On occasion, I have used my imagination to set the scene and add atmosphere. Key facts and events, however, remain unchanged.

Their journeys may have ended but their voices are remembered with love and affection.

Introduction

Both Lydia and Guydon (beloved parents of my sister, Eldar, and I) are sadly no longer with us. Guydon passed away on 12th April 2017 and Lydia three years later on 17th April 2020. Both suffered from terminal cancers at the end of their lives at the age of 83 respectively.

Listening to my mother's mellifluous voice on the tape recorder, reminds me of how I had forgotten who Lydia was during those last weeks of her life, when she was unwell. Her speech had become thick, slow and claggy, gluey and viscid. I was so overwhelmed in dealing with her illness and her deterioration that I seemed to have forgotten everything else about her. The disease took over her life, our relationship and the little time we had left together. We became engulfed and lost within that terrible fog of cancer. All else seemed to be swept away.

Listening to her voice on the tape reconnects me with her and brings her back to me. Lydia's story comes to life, once more, as the words tumble out of her.

Memories are often evoked by food. I made an almond cake today which my mother, Lydia, always made for birthdays and Passover. It is a recipe that goes back to my maternal grandmother's early life in Poland and her love of sweet delicacies. I was told that her mother (my great- grandmother Chana) made the most heavenly cakes and pastries! This recipe (see appendix 1) comes from that time. It is a beautifully simple cake made with only three ingredients and filled with a layer of home- made chocolate mousse! Irresistible and unforgettable!

My thoughts turn towards remembering Inga (a Jewish girl from Germany) who was taken in by my maternal grandparents

(Edzia and Ilia) in 1939 for a brief time. On the tape recording, my mother barely whispers her name and I can just about catch it. The recollection is so fragile. Inga's name could evaporate or break up like a weak radio signal at any moment. No sooner uttered, her name becomes a dying spark. She was about 12 years old when she came to stay with my mother's family in Brussels. My mother must have been only 3 years old at the time. Jewish families living in Germany were looking to place their children in safe homes away from the persecution of the Nazis which, after *Kristallnacht* [The Night of Broken Glass, 9th-10th November 1938], changed everything. This large-scale and organised violence against German Jews would mark the beginning of the Holocaust. Jews were physically attacked, their businesses looted and nearly 300 synagogues were set fire to. Thirty thousand Jewish males were rounded up and sent to concentration camps. The Night of Broken Glass refers to the shattered glass that littered the streets after the vandalism and destruction of Jewish- owned businesses, synagogues and homes. In the aftermath of *Kristallnacht,* the Nazi regime rapidly enacted many anti- Jewish laws and edicts.

Inga did not stay long with the family in Brussels, however, as they too would shortly be faced with the same predicament and would need to go into hiding to preserve their own lives. By chance, I recently came across a picture of Inga as I was scouring through old photograph albums. On the back of it my mother had made a note: *Inga was killed by American tank.* She had made it through the war and returned to Brussels, only to be tragically run over by an American tank on the day of liberation.

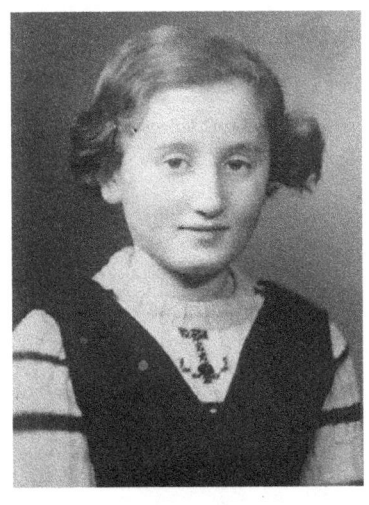

Sweet Inga

My maternal grandmother, Edwarda Szklarzowna, had kept all the members of her own family alive during the Second World War by her innate instincts, quick-wittedness and courage. She was a pragmatic woman who did not hesitate to make difficult decisions based on the realities she saw clearly before her. She saved herself, her mother (Chana), her daughter (Lydia) and her husband (Ilia) from death at the hands of the Nazis, who invaded Belgium in May 1940. This came at great personal cost to herself, as she was left broken by the end of the war, her nerves dangling like burnt-out wires.

As the tape runs, I hear the swish of the cigarette lighter and a pause before my mother carries on with her story.

For my mother, post- war liberation was first associated with freshly baked white bread, chocolate and chewing gum. But there would be many stories to tell before this euphoric moment.

Part 1 Edwarda's Story

The family saga must begin with my maternal grandmother's story who left a memoir about her remarkable life. The following is based on those memories and what she told me during many long hours of conversation. We would be transported to other times and places, only to realise that it was getting late by the shadows creeping into the room. She bestowed a precious gift to her family: the gift of remembering and telling.

Russia, family and feathered hats

Edwarda Szklarzowna, affectionately called Edzia by her family and friends, was born on 15th January 1914 in Warsaw, Poland (then part of the Russian empire), the year The First World War broke out. She was the youngest daughter of a Jewish family who were to seek their fortune in Russia. Her sister, Helene (Hela), was five years her senior. Edzia's father (David Szklarz) was an astute and successful businessman, who manufactured and sold exquisite hats to the aristocratic ladies of Moscow and St. Petersburg. These highly fashionable and expensive accessories were adorned with exotic feathers, their iridescent colours catching the light and capturing Edzia's fascination as a young child.

After leaving Warsaw as a baby, Edzia spent the first five years of her life in Ekaterinoslav (now known as Dnipro), a city in Ukraine (which was then part of Russia), where David had established his millinery business. The family enjoyed a lavish lifestyle whilst business boomed. The two sisters only knew a life of luxury and comfort. They wanted for nothing. Elegant evening dresses and fur stoles hung in their mother's armoire. Fine leather goods and silk scarves were tucked away in rose-scented drawers. Their mother's diamond earrings dazzled in the candlelight. Perfume bottles, a silver vanity set and a collection of trinket boxes inlaid with mother of pearl, tortoiseshell and enamel were arranged on her dressing table. The girls played for hours with exquisite dolls in front of a flickering marble fireplace. The dolls' pretty faces were hand-painted; they wore white lace dresses and soft leather boots with ivory buttons. There was a brightly painted puppet theatre with an assortment of hand-carved marionettes which opened up endless possibilities for the imagination.

A beautiful perambulator, intended for the third child, remained empty in the hallway. The poor infant did not survive long after birth. So Edzia played with the pram, placing her dolls inside it or asking to be pushed around in it herself.

The family had three servants to attend to their every need: the cook (a very large woman with folds of ample, soft, doughy flesh who sat upon two or three chairs like a pink powder puff), a nanny and a housekeeper. Cabinets were filled with fine glassware and silver cutlery. The windows in their large apartment were draped in heavy silks and velvets, insulating the rooms from icy chills and drafts. On the sideboard, the silver candlesticks shimmered and reflected against dark, polished mahogany furniture, upholstered in sumptuous fabrics. The walls of their elegant apartment were papered in rich red and gold patterned damasks. Parquet flooring swept through the plush rooms, as dark and shiny as polished ebony, giving off a subtle scent of warm, fragrant beeswax. Crystal chandeliers sparkled and cascaded like diamond fountains, suspended from magnificently high ceilings with intricately moulded cornices. Hela played the piano, singing Russian melodies in her sweet voice, which trailed and echoed through the grand interconnecting rooms of the apartment. The servants kept the fires going all day long. Edzia's mother, Chana, spent her days perfecting delicious pastries and cakes. A more charmed life could not have been imagined.

Hela was a headstrong and opinionated girl who was frequently outspoken. She was physically robust and advanced for her age. She might be described as a somewhat precocious child and it was not unusual for her to receive a slap from her father for impertinence. Edzia described her as being very intelligent and having a sharp mind. Edzia, on the other hand, was a delicate and often sickly child. She was underdeveloped and small for her age, quietly spoken and timid. She suffered from a series of illnesses which plagued her throughout her childhood. Despite being wrapped up from top to toe in furs, Edzia suffered from poor circulation. She developed agonisingly painful chilblains and remembered the blood oozing from her swollen, itching hands and feet. She would scream in despair and be given hot baths to soothe her discomfort. The harsh Russian winters exposed her to freezing conditions and unrelenting winds which cut into your eyes and face like blades of steel. She caught double pneumonia and had continuous bouts of bronchitis which meant that she would spend a great deal of time convalescing at home. Penicillin had not yet been discovered so the only treatment available was the cupping method, whereby heated glass cups were placed directly on the chest and back to draw out the infection or inflammation. Edzia cried out with displeasure during these treatments. David appeased her with gifts and chocolates.

Edzia experienced considerable ill health during much of her early childhood and, at times, her life seemed to teeter on the edge. If it were not for her mother's delectable pastries, she would have wasted away, as she could only be tempted with these delicacies. She would never forget the taste of her mother's fine cooking and delicious cakes which she savoured all her life. She would continue to suffer from chilblains for many years to come until her marriage to Ilia Chapiro in Brussels on 1st August 1936.

She remembered with deep and lasting nostalgia, the glowing and polished brass samovar which provided the family with a supply of hot water (morning, noon and evening) to make *zavarka* tea which was poured into glass cups held in silver holders called *podstakannik*. The samovar would be prepared by a servant early in the morning, before the family stirred. She would feed the inner pipe with sticks of lit firewood or burning charcoal until a beautiful flame flickered strong and steady, heating up the surrounding water contained in the body of the samovar. A filled teapot was set atop to steep. The samovar was a glint of sun through the long, dark, cruel and relentless Russian winters. It shone like a gold disc in the darkness of winter. The freshly made tea emitted a steamy, fragrant aroma with a hint of spice. The tea was so precious that it was locked inside a tea caddy. The sight of the shining samovar every morning on the sideboard made Edzia very happy.

Edzia always looked up to Hela, her elder sister, and followed her every word. Hela, unlike Edzia, had a strong and commanding voice, just like their father. Hela was often in conflict with her father, as they were both strong-willed and stubborn.

David Szklarz was a man of imposing physical stature, strength and energy. He wore small, round spectacles and always dressed in dark suits. He walked with a cane. Edzia recalled an incident where he had slammed his cane down on the table and demanded of an associate: '*Your money or your life!*' This made a lasting and deep impression on her mind. He exacted respect from everyone and he was a shrewd businessman. To Edzia, he always seemed to be shouting at the top of his voice, when in fact, he simply spoke in a strong and commanding tone. She grew to be somewhat fearful of him, never fully understanding him until much later, when she realised that there had been a deeply sentimental and tender side to his nature. During the earlier years of her life, she had considered him to be a domineering, demanding and despotic figure; her heart hardened towards him. She had admired her mother for handling David's fits of anger with such calmness. In fact, she had always revered and adored her mother above anyone else. She considered her a martyr in putting up with David's darker moods. Edzia took against her father and always sided with her mother and sister. She considered Chana to be the most patient and enduring of wives: putting up with David's bursts of temper with admirable collectedness and gentleness. Edzia became totally devoted to Chana later on. She hadn't realised that she had always been the apple of her father's eye and occupied a special place in his heart. Later on in her life, Edzia deeply regretted that she had misjudged and misunderstood David for so many years. But this awareness only dawned on her when it was already too late and caused her much sorrow.

The fortunes of the Szklarz family were about to change dramatically. Political unrest would eventually lead to the Russian Revolution of 1917 and the family would be forced to flee their adopted home and leave their once successful business behind them for good. As the revolution gathered pace and sentiment against wealthy capitalists and Jews gained momentum, the family found themselves caught up in an increasingly perilous situation. There came a point where they were in fear for their lives from Bolshevik, Menshevik and Cossack attacks. The Cossacks had a particularly savage reputation. With charging horses and poised swords, they did not hesitate to kill. They seemed to come from another world and filled Edzia's mind with terrifying images of brutality and destruction. The family tried to keep a low profile and would often be forced to go into hiding during these uncertain and chaotic times. Edzia remembered spending long hours in damp, freezing cellars wrapped in furs and blankets until the danger had passed. During these episodes, her chilblains worsened. She suffered acutely from the freezing conditions.

Chana became increasingly distressed as the situation around the family intensified, becoming more confusing, chaotic and violent with each passing day. No one knew who was who anymore and no one could be trusted. Chana was terrified of the Bolsheviks and begged David to hide their money and jewellery. He concealed their possessions inside some empty milk churns which he then placed in the cellar amongst the sacks of potatoes, coal, washing basins and scrubbing brushes. A few days later, when things had settled, David went down to the cellar to retrieve the money and jewellery. To his astonishment, he discovered that the money was missing! Luckily, the jewellery had not been touched. The police were notified and began their investigations. All of the servants were questioned. There was great drama and many a tear was shed! They swore, under oath, that they were innocent of any wrongdoing.

A few weeks after this event, it was brought to David's attention that the fortunes of the poor, wretched woman, Olga Leskova, whose job it was to scrub the pots and pans in the scullery, had suddenly taken a turn for the better. She was dressed in smart clothes and had a new pair of shoes. She boasted to the other servants that she had decorated her room with wallpaper. The police searched her quarters in the basement and found money stashed away behind some loosened bricks in the wall and inside sacks of white flour, a luxury which was very hard to come by then. They also discovered half a dozen pairs of new shoes. The miserable woman was arrested immediately and thrown into jail. What remained of the money was returned to Edzia's family.

Normality resumed for a short while and the incident was soon forgotten about until the Bolsheviks returned and released all of the prisoners from jail. Olga Leskova returned to the Szklarz home, shaking her fists and shouting from the street, threatening that David would pay dearly for his actions now that the

Bolsheviks had gained the upper hand. She swore there would be nowhere for the family to hide. They would be hunted down like animals!

The family became fearful. They left their beautiful apartment and stayed with some friends, lying low for a while. David was a wanted man as a capitalist and his life was under threat. It was during their stay with these friends that an incident occurred which Edzia never forgot. Two Cossacks were on the rampage nearby, pillaging everything in sight. With lightning speed, all the members of the household (including the children and servants) scrambled to grab whatever they could lay their hands on in order to make the most ear- splitting and deafening noise possible. Pots and pans were beaten upon, tables were struck with cutlery, chairs and crockery smashed to pieces as they shouted and cried out like wild beasts. The Cossacks fled. The ploy had been successful. However, everyone was hoarse for many days after.

Shortly after this incident, Olga Leskova's body was found floating in the river, half eaten by starving dogs! It was said that she had been killed by the Bolsheviks as a traitor.

Edzia and her family finally returned to their apartment. But it would not be for long.

No more feathered hats, the beginning of an epic journey & a young girl saves her father's life

David's hat manufacturing business collapsed. There was no longer any demand for sophisticated and expensive accessories. Communist ladies had no need for such frivolities. The family's comfortable life in Russia came to an end as chaos erupted and the noose tightened around them. It was too dangerous to remain and David made preparations for their departure.

They would, eventually, return to Warsaw in 1919. However, it took them many months to get there and their journey was not without incident or near catastrophe. As a capitalist and Jew, David was a wanted man. Nevertheless, the Szklarz family began their journey with hope.

During this period of great political upheaval and turmoil, there was very little public transport available. They ended up leaving Russia on a cattle train, headed towards Odessa where they hoped to cross the Black Sea to Constantinople. The family made themselves as comfortable as they could, sitting on piles of suitcases amidst bales of hay on the straw scattered floor of the cattle truck. Edzia described the fear on their faces and inside each one of their hearts. Every time she and Hela saw soldiers carrying rifles, they burst into tears whilst the adults' hearts were in their mouths. The train seemed to advance at a snail's pace over the immense distance that needed to be traversed. Edzia peered through a crack in the cattle car. The world beyond seemed so strange. They made their way sluggishly through a vast and seemingly endless expanse of flat and empty land devoid of any living thing: not a soul, beast or tree in sight. She thought they were at the end of the world. A red disc hung in the white sky.

At some point, the train suddenly ground to a halt in the middle of the empty Russian landscape. The family had no idea where they were. The ground was lightly dusted in crystallised snow which the wind whipped up into powdery clouds, like swirling, dancing ghosts. The doors slid open and armed soldiers ordered all of the men off the train. The order was given for Edzia's father to be shot on the spot. Friends of the family travelling with them at the time acted swiftly and bribed the driver to hold the train back. Chana passed out with the shock. The adults anxiously gathered around her. During the commotion and whilst everyone was distracted, Hela wasted no time in taking her chance and sprang into action. If it had not been for her quick thinking, irrepressible nature and determination, their father would have been lost to them forever. Hela's resolve to save his life was unshakeable and propelled her to act immediately. There was not a moment to lose and she did not hesitate for a second. She grabbed little Edzia's hand before climbing off the train and marched over to the officer in charge, pleading with him to release her father. She spun a yarn about herself and her little sister being left destitute and orphaned without him. They had no mother, nowhere to go, no family and no money. She tried to appeal to his human side. She asked him whether he had any children of his own and did they still have their mother? He looked away from Hela for a moment in order to reflect upon her words and collect his thoughts. When he finally turned to face her there were tears in his eyes and he assured her that all would be well. He promptly gave the order for the release of not only David but the other detainees as well. Did any of those men have any idea that they had been saved by the bold actions of a plucky eight-year old girl who had not, for one moment, given up hope or surrendered to fear?

> 'Hope for life does not expire,' Edzia wrote in her memoirs. 'I can say this because I would experience this several times during the course of my life…'

Finally, David and Hela got back on the train and it continued on its way. Edzia described her father suffering from crippling stomach cramps after this incident. Her mother recovered from her fainting fit but she had become overwhelmed by listlessness. She had turned deathly pale; her eyes dull, empty, lifeless pools.

David was feeling so ill that he had no option but to jump off the train in order to relieve himself. He was confident that he could catch up with the slow- moving train. However, no sooner did he jump off then the train began to gather pace! He could not catch them up and they feared they had lost him for the second time! Chana and the girls disembarked at the next station (many miles and hours later) and waited for David. Finally, after a few days, the family were re-united once again and their hearts sang with joy!

Edzia was only three or four years old at the time. She had experienced so much already in her short life. The train pushed on into the faceless and chilling wind. The family were travelling towards an unknown future. They were trapped within a maelstrom of world events: The First World War, the Ukranian Nationalists fighting for independence and a civil war between the Reds (Bolsheviks) and Whites (Tsarists). They would have to navigate and dodge their way through this hazardous landscape. The route home would be long and circuitous.

Much later on, Edzia expressed sympathy for the predicament of the Russian people. As a small child, she had been unaware of the terrible poverty suffered by millions. She did not blame them for their unrest or for their desperate actions.

An earthquake and soaring minarets

The family did, eventually, embark on a boat at the port of Odessa and from here they made their way to Constantinople. On the way, Hela revealed to her younger sister that money had been secretly sewn into the lining of their fur hoods and muffs and their mother's large fur collar. Their father had had their suitcases, hair brushes and vanity cases fitted with secret compartments to hide jewellery. She must tell no one, not a soul. Nervously, Edzia couldn't resist feeling the padding inside her fur muff, which crackled like paper or small, stifled fireworks.

On finally reaching Constantinople, their ship was unable to enter the port. A smaller boat was sent out to collect the passengers. A gangplank was made ready connecting the two vessels. But when Edzia saw the sight of this narrow walkway stretching high above the open sea, she was seized with crippling fear and panic. The sea below looked dark and menacing, lapping against the sides of the boats like the grasping tentacles of a sea monster. Hela, reading the expression on her little sister's face, firmly and confidently took hold of her hand and led her across the ramp to safety.

The family spent a few weeks in Constantinople, awaiting transport for the next leg of their epic journey to Poland. David went to the port every day, enquiring whether there was a ship that could take them onwards. During their stay, Edzia remembered that there was an earthquake. After the tremor, a pattern of fine cracks appeared on the wall of their hotel room, a picture had fallen and the furniture had shifted. Against a backdrop of crimson splashed skies and a hypnotic call to prayer, the silhouettes of soaring minarets and majestic domes inhabited the girls' imaginations.

Finally, they set sail for Poland. The seas were rough and the ship tossed from side to side. Everyone was very sick, apart from David. Chana clasped the railings of the ship until her knuckles turned white and she became thoroughly drenched.

Finally, Poland

When the family finally arrived in Poland in 1919, friends and family were incredulous that they were still alive, believing them to have been killed by the Bolsheviks. However, it would soon be a case of 'Out of the frying pan into the fire'. The newly independent Poland would shortly enter a war with the Soviet Union which reached Warsaw in 1920. On this occasion, Poland prevailed.

A train wagon load of tobacco was awaiting the Szklarz family in Poland, having been sent on ahead by David. In order to avoid detection by the Russian authorities, he had made sure the paperwork could not be traced back to him by putting it under the name of a Polish officer. According to Edzia, it was worth a fortune (roubles were worthless by that time) and would enable the family to begin their new lives in Poland. Later on, Edzia recognised how clever her father had been in purchasing the tobacco. He had found a way of safeguarding some of their assets in the midst of politically uncertain and economically turbulent times. This would enable him to set up his new business: a knitwear factory in Warsaw.

Whilst David organised their accommodation in Warsaw, the family stayed with grandparents who lived in the countryside. Life in rural Poland was not what they were accustomed to. Initially,

Edzia experienced this way of life as miserable, primitive and pitiful. The houses were wooden structures which she found to be small, dark, dismal, dank, cold and drafty. Simple country food was basic and unappetising to her taste. People were poorly dressed. She could not speak or understand a word of Polish, which meant that she could not communicate with her relatives or other children. The smell of pungent horse dung hung on the air, attracting swarms of flies while carts piled high with hay slowly made their way up and down the dirt roads. These were not scenes the young Edzia was accustomed to. Thus far she had only known a life of comfort, servants and delectable patisserie! Edzia never forgot the sight of a poor crippled woman in the village who had no legs. She got around by supporting herself on her hands and then swung herself forwards on the ground. Sometimes, she would be carted around in a wheelbarrow. One day, she entered the house of Edzia's grandparents. Edzia was so terrified by the sight of this woman with filthy, raven- black, matted hair that she climbed up onto the kitchen table and refused to come down until the woman had left, her face streaming with tears! Who knows what the poor woman must have thought but Edzia was very young at the time. What a nightmare this scene had been for her as a young child at the age of five years old! However, when the time came to leave the village, she almost regretted it. She had grown accustomed to the people and simple life she found there.

A new life in Warsaw

Finally, Chana and her two daughters left for Warsaw where they moved into a newly built and furnished bungalow, equipped with every comfort a well to do family could wish for. This was all made possible thanks to David's foresight in purchasing the train wagon load of tobacco which he was able to sell for a very substantial sum of money once in Poland. Edzia was sent to school, not knowing any Polish and never having been to school before! On her first day, the children laughed at her for not understanding anything. How cruel children can be towards the misfortunes of others! Edzia felt ashamed and cried. It was a drama for a while until she got to grips with this new language, which she soon did, as it resembled Russian in some ways and things soon started to improve. However, she was never top of her class. She struggled with reading, writing and arithmetic. She was, however, extremely clever with her hands and applied herself to needlework classes with skill. She sewed with neat and precise stitches like a little elf. She could soon turn her hand to making small clothes for her dolls, soft toys and pet animals! She demonstrated great ability in her gymnastic class also. She was naturally graceful and poised, displaying perfect balance and co-ordination. She was petite, supple and sprightly. When offered language classes in either German or French, Edzia did not hesitate in choosing the latter. She considered French and Russian to be the two most beautiful languages of all. Later on, she would wonder at her rejection of the German language. Had it been a premonition of what was to come or simple intuition? Her acquisition of French would, unwittingly, prepare her for a future life in Belgium (a country that she would take to from the very instant) and serve her well. But she was not to have known any of these things at the time. Her instincts seemed to show her the way even at that early time, which would turn out to always be the case.

The family kept a menagerie of animals in the courtyard of their bungalow. There were dogs (deeply adored by Edzia), chickens, pigeons (who were stalked and hunted down by the cat) and a cockerel. When a bad-tempered grandmother came to stay with them, the cockerel chased her all around the courtyard, seeming to sense that she was not a very kindly woman. When kittens arrived, Edzia was in heaven! She spent hours gently grooming their soft fur with her mother's silver brushes and combs, made them pretty collars out of black velvet ribbons with silver bells sewn on, spoiled them with cream served from the best China saucers, petted and played with them all day long. She would simply refuse to go to school on some days, insisting that she would be far better off staying at home with her beloved pets. Her dogs were far more important to her than school. And instead of completing her homework, she would play with the little chicks on her desk.

Eventually, Edzia spoke Polish well enough to be able to play with the other children and David's business seemed to be thriving. The family, once again, enjoyed a peaceful, secure, well-organised and prosperous existence.

Ham

David was a pragmatic man and had absolutely no interest in religious matters whatsoever. When he took his daughters out, he bought them ham. Edzia remembered thickly cut slices wrapped in waxy paper. The girls would devour the deliciously sweet ham on their way home, as their mother would not allow it in the house. However, when the physician recommended the consumption of ham to boost Edzia's strength, her mother could not argue with him and she finally permitted it in the house. She was extremely careful, however, not to use the dish the ham was served on for any other foods. Edzia enjoyed eating ham for the rest of her life.

God, religion and Christmas

Edzia remained intolerant towards any form of religious fanaticism all of her life. She grew up without believing in the existence of a god. And later on, at a critical moment in history when her people had needed their God most, she saw that they were utterly abandoned to their fate. God, who is supposed to be the protector, did not do his work. This was proof enough to her mind that he did not exist.

During Christmas in Warsaw, the family would decorate a beautiful and large tree. It gave great pleasure to the children. Edzia's family were not religious, by any stretch of the imagination, and permitted such traditions for the children's pure enjoyment. Chana prepared traditional and celebratory meals to mark Jewish holidays and festivals but without religious overtones. David was altogether indifferent to religion.

Parties

David was as generous and indulgent as ever. For every birthday, a magnificent party would be thrown. Guests were treated to rich and delicious foods. They sunk their silver pastry forks into soft, sweet cakes. They drank champagne and sipped lemon tea. Hela might play the piano and sing one of the sweet Russian melodies in her lovely voice. Girls with pretty ribbons in their hair and lace dresses ran around excitedly with smartly suited boys. There was laughter and merriment. Expensive gifts were purchased: a gold watch, a string of pearls, a silver marcasite broach, a mink stole, a ring set with precious stones, gold chains and amber beads. Life was marvellous once again for a time, just as it had been in Ekaterinoslav during the heyday of the hat manufacturing years. David's new business venture was going well.

Hela falls in love

At the age of 15, Hela announced that she had fallen in love! Hela had already confided in her younger sister. Edzia remembered watching Hela applying lipstick and pinning up her hair to make herself look older and more sophisticated before meeting her sweetheart on a secret rendezvous. Her lover was a man 10 years her senior! Kuba came from a poor family and worked as a clerk in David's business. He was clever and ambitious, wanting to make something of himself. David went wild with fury when he found out and both parents forbade the liaison to continue due to the age difference. They shouted at Hela and warned her against the folly of her actions in no uncertain terms. But nothing would deter her. She dug her heels in and would not be dissuaded. Remember, this is the same girl who had saved her father's life by deterring an officer from shooting him when she was only eight years old! Hela declared that she would have Kuba or no one at all! Edzia sided with her sister, of course. Even David was defeated (in the end) by his daughter's determination, obstinacy and sheer pig headedness. Reluctantly, the parents gave consent for Hela to become engaged at the age of 16. Two years later, she was married to Kuba.

Hela should have heeded her parents' caution, as Kuba's true character would only be completely revealed later on.

A splendid wedding

David arranged a marvellous wedding for the couple, with no expense spared. Hundreds of guests were invited and it was the talk of Warsaw! Many beautiful dresses were purchased for the occasion. Ladies were perfectly coiffed and bejewelled. Men wore elegant morning suits. Waiters floated up and down the aisles in tailcoats, balancing silver trays laden with champagne- filled fluted glasses upon white gloved fingertips. A sumptuous banquet with countless courses was enjoyed. Wafts of perfume and cigar smoke lingered on the air. A table laden with magnificent wedding gifts caught everyone's eye. The finest bed linen, goose feather eiderdowns, crystal glasses, dishes, bowls, vases and water jugs, a canteen of silver cutlery, a superb dinner service, silver caddy spoons, copper pans, a pewter coffee set, hand embroidered tablecloths trimmed with lace, a silver cruet set, cut crystal salts, a crystal and silver butter set, silver trays, champagne coasters, claret jugs and decanters, a wine cooler, silver candlesticks, porcelain figurines, silver cigarette boxes and the list goes on. Edzia had never seen such opulence and magnificence. She may have dreamed that, one day, she too would have a wedding like this. She was 15 years old.

David, as bounteous as ever, had installed the newly- weds in a fully furnished and equipped apartment. A maid had been hired in order to make everything perfect for them. They even had a record player and radio, great luxuries which only the very wealthy could afford. David had bought Kuba his own knitwear machines, hoping that this would encourage him to set up independently. Instinct told David that he needed to keep Kuba at bay with regards to his own business interests. David had, against his better judgement, given in to his eldest daughter's demands and would pay dearly for this error in the future (in spite of his best efforts to avoid catastrophe). The knitwear machines would become central to the story of David's eventual downfall.

Sweet times

As an adolescent, Edzia enjoyed a carefree life of pleasure in Warsaw, unaware that her father's business was falling into a steady decline. As time went by, she was permitted more independence. She was tired of being the baby of the family! She welcomed the opportunity to grow up and feel a sense of freedom. No longer did she have to share a room with her sister! This was a particularly lovely and sweet time in her life. Her social life burgeoned with blossoming friendships and innocent romances. There were theatre trips to enjoy, cafe and cinema outings, exciting new ideas to discuss, dances and country rambles. Edzia's wardrobe was filled with fashionable dresses, pretty blouses and skirts, hats and jackets with fur trimmed collars, handmade shoes with small heels perfect for hopping on and off the trams and sauntering down the wide and elegant boulevards arm in arm with friends. A pair of kid leather gloves lay on her dressing table along with an arrangement of perfume bottles and enamelled compacts. A blissful time for this young girl on the cusp of womanhood.

The tide is turning

At the same time, David found himself under mounting financial pressure. The political regime in Poland in the 1920's was becoming increasingly antisemitic in a manner similar to that of Nazi Germany in the 1930's. Edzia had witnessed orthodox Jews forcibly having their beards cut off in the street. Jews were being targeted with punitive taxes which made subsistence virtually impossible. The relentless economic discrimination against the Jews left David on the brink of bankruptcy. He was forced to sell some property in order to keep going. Eventually, he was faced with no alternative but to relocate his family once more, this time to Brussels, Belgium. Perhaps David had established some business contacts there already.

At this point, David desperately wanted to disassociate himself from Kuba who turned out to be an unscrupulous, double dealing and dishonest man who was robbing David blind. Edzia and Chana were in ignorance of this because David kept the gravity of the situation from them. However, he thought that by relocating his family to Belgium, he would be able to distance himself from Kuba and make a clean break. Chana objected strongly to the idea of leaving Hela and Kuba behind in Poland. She simply wouldn't hear of it. Once again, David gave in to his family's wishes (against his better judgement).

The knitwear machines were packed up and sent on to Brussels. With a heavy heart, David locked up his workshop which would fall within the walls of the Warsaw ghetto (1940-3) by which time David had died and Edzia (living in Brussels as a young married woman with an infant) found herself having to face the unthinkable. Their bungalow was left behind for good. David was forever swimming against the tide, it seemed.

The family never returned to Warsaw or Poland again. Had they done so, they would not have recognised it because Warsaw would be the target of a huge and unrestricted aerial bombardment by the Luftwaffe in 1939, during the Nazi invasion of Poland. Apart from military facilities, civilian facilities such as waterworks, hospitals, market places and schools were also targeted, resulting in heavy human casualties. Warsaw was heavily bombed again towards the end of the war.

Beautiful Brussels

Edzia was 16 years old when the family finally arrived in Brussels, Belgium in 1930. She immediately took to this lovely country and its language. However, her life would be completely different to the one she had left behind in Poland. The Szklarz family had lost their fortune and, to add to this, David had been swindled out of a significant sum of money by an associate of his whom he had entrusted to transfer money from Poland to Belgium. They had to start all over again in the midst of the Great Depression, and Edzia would have to work for the first time in her life. Servants and luxuries were a thing of the past. David, who could not speak the language and did not understand how business worked in this part of the world, struggled to adapt and leant heavily on his youngest daughter who had adjusted to their new life and knew something of the language which she had begun learning at school in Poland.

The family moved into a modest house in one of the more popular districts of Brussels. Edzia soon found herself not only working for her father in the knitwear business, but also having to look after the house and deal with the weekly mountains of laundry!

Chana shopped for groceries and cooked. Otherwise, she rarely left the house. With each passing day, she became more bitter and sour. Her beautiful clothes no longer fitted her. They hung in the wardrobe smelling of mothballs. She became drab and dowdy and aged quickly. She didn't seem to care about her appearance anymore and let herself go. She soon became unwell, developing diabetes. However, she continued making her beautiful cakes and pastries.

Edzia did not shy away from hard work, in spite of her frail constitution. She was keen to help her father as much as she could (even though she was not close to him) understanding the financial strain he was under. No longer a young man with the energy, confidence and know-how of his previous life, David struggled to make things work. He was under a great deal of pressure which made him suffer from bouts of illness and weakness. He had always been such a strong man in the eyes of his family. They did not understand the implications of his poor health and paid little attention to it. In fact, there was much that they did not understand at this point.

Edzia adapted to her new role with readiness and good will, although she found it hard. She was pragmatic and realistic; she did not shy away from hard work. She simply got on with what needed to be done without complaint or regret. Her life of comfort and ease was a thing of the past now. Her father needed her support and she had to look after her mother. She had a sense of responsibility towards her family who were central to her life. She had always been adept with her hands and practical. She learned to master the different knitwear machines quickly and skilfully. There were machines for cutting, sewing, buttonhole making and seams. She worked alongside David's employees, who became her friends. They were all very fond of their employer's attractive, petite young daughter with her lively, mischievous and warm personality! Edzia had a sharp little nose, green eyes and long, luxuriant copper- red hair which she plaited into very becoming styles. (Her Arian looks would serve her well later on in the story during the Nazi occupation of Belgium). She was a talented dressmaker and seamstress, making her own clothes or re- modelling old ones. She always dressed stylishly and fashionably. She was elegant and chic. Her work colleagues told her that everything she touched turned to gold, meaning that she could apply herself to anything and it always turned out well! And as time passed, she grew ever more confident in speaking French and more settled in this new country for which she developed a great fondness.

The musings of a young girl on the cusp of womanhood

At the age of 16, Edzia's life had changed dramatically. She was cut off from her friends in Poland and was now always in the company of her family. It became claustrophobic for her. She longed to meet people of her own age. Her only entertainment, outings to the fairground. She had brought with her, from Poland, a little notebook full of her friends' signatures and farewell messages to remember them by. During the evenings, in the privacy of her own room and when all of the day's chores were done, she would bring this little notebook out, read the names and affectionate words from her old friends, see their faces once again and reminisce.

She remembered her private tutor, Juliusz Krelman, who was a student at the university. This young man became a close friend.

He came to the house in Warsaw almost every day to help her with her studies, as she had never been a 'star pupil' at school. She was a young adolescent at the time. She learned many things from him and they even went on cinema outings together. They had a real friendship. Edzia insisted that each one of them pay for their own ticket (although it was the convention for the man to pay) as it was important for her to feel free and independent.

She remembered inviting her good friend Tola (who was 17 at the time and lived in the countryside) to stay with her in Warsaw for a week. One evening, they went out to the theatre. Edzia promised Chana that they would be back before midnight. Unfortunately, the show finished later than Edzia had expected and although she was seized with panic, she also wanted to impress Tola and show her how grown up she was. By the time the two friends got home, it was well past midnight. Chana was waiting for them and as soon as she saw her daughter, she hit the roof and gave Edzia quite a slap in front of her friend. Luckily, her father was asleep at the time as he would have been even angrier!

After a week in Warsaw, Edzia was invited to stay with Tola's family in the countryside. She was presented to Tola's brother, Ludwik, who was 20 years old, charming, attractive and tall! Knowing of Edzia's arrival he had bought tickets for a dance. Ludwik and Edzia danced together all night and made a very handsome couple! Everyone stopped to admire them and applauded. Edzia felt quite shy about it all but Ludwik assured her that nothing could be more natural. He was quite protective towards her. Edzia was introduced to the other guests as, 'My friend from the city,' which made her really proud. After the dance, the three friends were in high spirits and linked arms all the way home, laughing and sliding on the thin ice under the glinting stars.

It turned out that Ludwik had taken quite a shine to Edzia. During a stay in Warsaw, he invited her out to chic cafes, evening strolls in the park and along the handsome boulevards of the city. However, he was always a gentleman in her presence, never taking advantage of her youth or innocence! He carried around with him a bamboo cane which, at the time, was the height of fashion and very expensive! He was quite the dandy! During one of their playful walks together, Edzia accidentally broke the cane. Ludwik seemed somewhat annoyed by this incident and became quite preoccupied with thoughts on how the cane should be repaired. Only a band of solid gold would do! Edzia came to the conclusion that he was an intolerable snob and her attitude towards him changed from that moment onwards. She teased him relentlessly. Yet, it would seem that he still remained keen on her and continued writing to her frequently.

> *'What a lovely, youthful, free time that had been. That is the kind of world that should always exist: a world devoid of envy, malice, danger and war. A world which allows everyone to realise their personal ambitions, whether they be intellectual, physical, artistic, professional or manual. A free world...'* Thus thought Edzia much later on in her life when she looked back on this time whilst writing her memoires.

Shortly after settling into their new home in Brussels, a piano arrived to the delight of the family! Now Hela could continue playing her sweet Russian melodies, her voice strong, tender and sentimental.

Etched within the deep furrows of Edzia's memory was a recollection of frozen lakes and white Russian winters. When she slept, heavy snow fell quietly upon the landscape of her dreams and a blisteringly bitter wind buffeted against her. Trains ploughed through deep snowdrifts at breakneck speed. Her dreams unfurled in silence, like white, satin ribbons.

Precious letters

Edzia received many letters from her friends back in Warsaw during her first few years in Brussels. She kept every single one of them and I have them in my possession today, as my mother did before me. There are many letters from Genia, her best friend from Poland. Genia's letters are written on small pieces of writing paper in the tiniest, neatest script. I imagine they are full of news and gossip. The envelopes are addressed to Mademoiselle Edzia Szklarz, 149 Rue de la Victoire, Bruxelles. The little pages are crammed full with Genia's exquisite handwriting. She seemed to have much to write about to her dear friend. I do not know what became of Genia, Tola, Ludwik, Juliusz, Henick, Jozef and the others who wrote to her and left their tender messages and drawings in her book of autographs.

In fact, I dread to think what became of these lovely and cherished young friends of Edzia's youth. Did they manage to escape the Nazi atrocities in Poland? If so, where did they go? If not, then we know only too well the fate of the Polish Jews during this most terrible of times: the massacres, pogroms, ghettos, deportations, labour and death camps. She never mentioned any of these friends to me, so I can only assume that none of them survived.

> *On the eve of the German occupation of Poland in 1939, 3.3 million Jews lived there. At the end of the war, approximately 380,000 Polish Jews remained alive, the rest having been murdered, mostly in the ghettos and the six death camps: Chelmo, Belzec, Sobibor, Treblinka, Majdanek and Auschwitz-Birkenau. (Yad Vashem. The World Holocaust Remembrance Centre. Murder of the Jews of Poland.)*

Chana's delectable pastries

Before setting out in the mornings, Edzia would raid the pantry where Chana stored all the freshly made pastries and cakes. Arriving at the knitwear workshop, she would share them out to the delight of her fellow workers. Returning home at the end of the day, she would announce to her mother that there were no more pastries left! Chana simply couldn't believe that her daughter had devoured them all by herself! So, in future, she hid them where they could not be found.

Edzia arrived at the workshop the next morning, empty handed. Her friends were very disappointed! Nevertheless, they had still purchased a lovely bouquet of flowers for her birthday! Edzia always remembered the affection and camaraderie between them.

Laundry days

The day Edzia dreaded the most was Laundry Day! The family had always relied on servants for this in the past. But their fortunes had turned and now the two sisters had no choice but to face this daunting task themselves! They took it in turns every week. Edzia found it exhausting. She surveyed the mountains of bed linen and clothing with trepidation. She scrubbed and washed until her poor hands bled and her nails broke. She was drenched in sweat by the end and trembled with the exertion. She was small in stature and not at all robust! Laundry days made her ill. After she had hung out the laundry to dry in the cellar, she would sit down on an old, rickety chair and light a cigarette. She held the cigarette between her shaking fingers, taking in a long and deep drag of smoke, which immediately calmed her nerves. She took a moment to look around her, taking in the gloomy atmosphere. A single shaft of light beamed down through a small side window covered in cobwebs. She watched the floating particles of dust. Edzia would become a lifelong smoker.

Soon, she became proficient enough in French to start reading novels, which she very much enjoyed although she had little time for these small pleasures.

Edzia adapted to life well in Belgium, a country she grew to like more and more as time passed. In spite of her weak disposition, she worked hard and never shied away from her duties and responsibilities. She was always steadfast in this. She had surprising stamina for one who had not been born strong. She looked to the future with youthful optimism and hope.

Edzia's turn to fall in love

When Edzia fell in love, that was it! One evening, her father brought home for dinner a travelling salesman of hosiery wares by the name of Ilia Chapiro. Edzia was immediately struck by his handsome, dark, mature good looks. Originally from Lithuania, he was 14 years older than her. She noted that his penetrating, warm, dark eyes followed her around the room like glowing lanterns. He sang Russian songs in a deep resonant voice which pierced through her heart like a spear. He captivated her with stories and adventures from his fascinating early life. He was utterly charming and she was bewitched, cast under his spell. He made her feel like a real woman, not just a slip of a girl. Her head was turned and there was no going back! She craved romance and a life of her own! She longed for some respite from the drudgery of everyday life with her family and work! Edzia's trim figure, auburn hair and sharp green eyes caught the attention of Ilia immediately. He was drawn to her energy and fire. It was not long before she gave herself to him freely. She felt happy!

All of this did not go unnoticed by David, who kept an ever-watchful eye on his youngest daughter. And when he asked her about her intentions with regards to Ilia, she had felt so awkward that she wished for the floor under her feet to swallow her up so that she could vanish!

Soon, there would be a rather hasty marriage. However, it would be nothing like Hela's wedding in Poland. It was a very modest affair for the immediate family only. There would be no lavish gifts or sumptuous reception party. Homemade food was prepared and one bottle of champagne was opened to toast the newly-weds and wish them a happy future! Edzia was now 22 years old and 6 months pregnant! Ilia was 36 years old.

Ilia Chapiro's story

On first meeting Edzia's family, Ilia had kept them awake late into the night by recounting the story of his youth (which will explain his attitude towards the invading Germans later on in the story).

Ilia was born on 1st October 1900, Kovno, Lithuania. At the age of 14, at the outbreak of the First World War in 1914, he was taken as a prisoner of war by the passing German army. How had this happened? Well might you ask.

Ilia had irrepressible curiosity as a boy; he found himself snooping around the military units and weapons of the German army who were stationed near his home town. However, one day, he was caught in the act. Despite pleading his innocence and revealing his age, he was not believed. The soldier saw before him a tall and well-built young man (not a boy) who had been acting suspiciously, therefore he must be a spy! He demanded to see Ilia's identity papers (which Ilia did not possess being too young). Hence, Ilia was ordered to present himself to the commanding officer the following morning. Despite protestations from his family, Ilia's curiosity got the better of him and he went. As a consequence of this, he ended up on the march with this German battalion, as a prisoner of war. At the time, he believed this to be the greatest adventure of his life!

They marched for many months across difficult terrain, having to endure freezing conditions. Ilia developed excruciatingly painful blisters. He slept in drafty barns or empty cattle trucks with only a thin blanket to shield him from the bitter cold. Abandoned train compartments were no better: the icy cold and damp chilled one to the bone. When no shelter was available, the marching army would bury themselves in dug out snow pits and fall asleep from sheer exhaustion. Despite the continuous hunger, cold and fatigue, Ilia had the exuberance of youth on his side. He admired the discipline of the German army! When they finally arrived at the barracks, they were issued with straw palliasses to sleep on: a luxury after enduring so much hardship!

Ilia's fluent Russian and knowledge of the German language eventually came to the notice of the elderly and kindly German Commandant who promoted him to the position of official translator. This afforded Ilia special privileges and he was immediately treated with respect by the other officers. In fact, he was allocated a room normally reserved for senior officials which came with the services of his own batman who addressed him submissively as 'Sir' every day. He prepared breakfast for Ilia each morning, cleaned his room, made up the bed and polished his boots. Ilia enjoyed the privileges of a high-ranking officer whilst in this position. He even had his own wardrobe and was issued with a smart khaki uniform which fitted him very well. On the right sleeve a red ribbon with the words 'Interpreter' was sewn on. The remaining prisoners of war (Russian, French and British) did not begrudge him this change in fortune and they bore him no ill will. Ilia noted that the German army was tolerant towards the Jewish prisoners of war who were allowed to practise their faith at the local synagogue on the Sabbath or other holy days. The Germans did not object or stand in their way.

In fact, this episode turned out to be one of the best times of his life. Musicians, artists and intellectuals were among the inmates of the prisoner of war camp. This led to the establishment of an orchestra and regular evening concerts. Cultural arrangements of a literary nature took place from which Ilia learned a great deal. As time passed, the Commandant (who had already taken a shine to Ilia) listened to his story. And this time he was believed. The Commandant decided the army was no place for such a bright young boy and invited him to Berlin to stay with his wife and children, where he could resume his education. Ilia could hardly believe his good luck and the dazzling opportunity presented before him. He accepted with alacrity and gratitude.

The Commandant arranged and paid for his passage to Berlin where his wife and children would be waiting for him. Ilia was given a comfortable room in their large and elegant house and was treated as their guest. A private tutor was hired to prepare Ilia for his entry to 'The Kaiser Friedrich Gymnasium' (private High School) where he received an excellent academic education paid for by the German Commandant, including books, stationery and school uniform. Ilia did well there, eventually passing all of his grammar school examinations. During this time in Berlin, he met other Jewish students whose well- established, professional families were perfectly assimilated within German society.

After some time had passed, Ilia had indeed become a real young man. He decided that he would take on some casual work so that he could support himself independently. Deeply thankful to the Commandant and his family for their patronage and kindness over the years, Ilia bade his farewells and started on this new chapter of his life. His benefactors wished him well and hoped that he would come to visit them often.

Berlin in the 1920s was the third largest city in the world; the centre of German culture and intellectual life. Many of Germany's most prominent writers, artists, academics and performers were based there. 'The Golden Twenties' was a vibrant period in the history of Berlin. It was known, worldwide, for its leadership in science, the humanities, music, film, architecture and design, higher education, government, diplomacy, industry and military affairs.

A sophisticated and innovative culture developed in and around Berlin turning it into a vibrantly cosmopolitan city.

Ilia fell in love with the Berlin of the 1920's. Who could not be enchanted by its style and sophistication and the intellectual buzz pulsating through this beautiful city? He had the highest regard for the German people and their culture. He visited the Berlin Opera House on many an occasion. He frequented cafes, cinemas, restaurants and theatres. He strolled up and down the city's avenues and boulevards, travelled on the trams that criss- crossed the city, soaking up the atmosphere of ease, tolerance, open-mindedness and freedom he found there.

Ilia supported himself by taking on various jobs. At one point, he found employment at a printer's press, then he found a position as a packer in a department store. He never remained long in one position, though. Together with a generous allowance from his family back home in Lithuania, he managed to save up a considerable amount of money which allowed him to purchase a beautiful suit, tailored from the finest cloth. He frequented restaurants and cafes, cinemas and concert halls, often with an attractive young lady on his arm. He enjoyed spending money liberally on pleasurable pursuits and indulged himself!

Eventually, Ilia joined the Medical Faculty of Berlin University to pursue his studies. And although he felt a deep attachment to Berlin and a sense of belonging there, he missed the Jewish atmosphere that he had been brought up in.

Because of these nostalgic feelings, Ilia became increasingly involved with Zionist organisations and activities. He became friends with the chief cantor at the Berlin synagogue and was able to introduce the congregation to Jewish songs every Sabbath. Apparently, he was thought to have a very pleasing voice which caught the ear of many! He was often invited into the home of a German Jewish family on a Seder night (Jewish ritual service and ceremonial dinner for the first or first two nights of Passover/Pesach) and was always warmly received.

Finally, a Zionist congress brought him to the fair city of Brussels on 25th April, 1925. He was so taken with the city that he decided to continue his medical studies there whilst attending French language classes.

In order to sustain this new venture, Ilia took on casual work, including a period working in a factory. He continued to be actively involved with Zionist movements in Brussels and had many contacts within its circles.

However, Ilia's intention to pursue his medical studies did not come to fruition. He was too unfocused and distracted. Truth be told, he was a bit of a dreamer (even a fantasist) and followed his whims all too easily, wherever they might take him. It might even be said that he had suffered from too much vanity. However, the need to earn money in order to subsist became a priority. The regular allowance he had come to depend on from his family back home in Lithuania was dwindling each month. He jumped from job to job, finding it impossible to stick at anything for any length of time. He had to be thrifty now, which did not appeal or come naturally to him! And that is how his path eventually crossed with David Szklarz, as a travelling salesman of hosiery wares.

Ilia never returned to Berlin. He married Edzia and in 1936 they had a beautiful little girl named Lydia born on 6th November of the same year.

Hela, Kuba and the birth of Harry

Hela and Kuba would eventually move into their own humble abode, as tensions within the family increased. In 1931 Edzia's nephew, Harry, was born. In his aunt's eyes, he was the loveliest and most intelligent child. Edzia loved to take him out for strolls in his perambulator, taking pleasure in allowing passers-by to imagine that he was her child. On the way, she would stop off to buy a bar of delicious Belgian chocolate.

At this time, Hela and Kuba were crying poverty. Chana made Edzia visit the young couple in secret (without David's knowledge) in order to supply them with weekly groceries (fish, chicken, fresh fruit and vegetables, cheese, milk) and other provisions, which they gladly accepted. Chana made sure they did not go without. At the same time, David was struggling to make the knitwear business profitable. In fact, he was losing money all the time and running up huge debts. This was the time of The Great Depression and he was affected badly by it. Kuba was surreptitiously building up his own business in direct competition to David, who was very well aware of this. What

David had no inkling about, though, was that he was also paying for Kuba's weekly grocery bills!

When Kuba demanded the return of a machine that had been gifted to him as a wedding gift, David hit the roof. Kuba had coaxed Edzia to speak to David on his behalf. She had never seen her father so enraged. She thought that he was going to throw one of the heavy, cone shaped bobbins at her. But no. How little she knew and understood her father at the time. In fact, he began to unscrew the machine from its bench. He called a taxi, threw the machine in with her and handed her the fare to Kuba's.

A heart attack, a hard heart and regret

Shortly after this incident, David had a heart attack. Edzia recalled watching his tall body slide down the wall and fall into a crumpled heap on the floor. David Szklarz, who had once been so invincible, a towering force of a man who did not suffer fools gladly; a man, whom his youngest daughter regarded as a tyrant and despot. The truth was that David had been devoted to his family. He had only wanted to provide a good life for them. Yes, he had been strong willed and had a forceful character. He had also been hard- working, courageous and intelligent. David was a self- made man, deserving admiration and respect for his achievements during times of opportunity as well as great challenge. And although he had enjoyed much success in the past as a talented business man, now, too many things were stacked against him.

However, Edzia's heart was still opposed to her father. It was only later (when truths had unravelled and her eyes were opened for the first time) that she saw the folly of her ways and how misguided she had been in judging her father so harshly.

David recovered from his heart attack but was left weakened and continued to suffer from bouts of ill health. He was faced with insurmountable financial problems which caused him great distress. It was emerging that Kuba had been poaching clients away from his father- in- law all this time. He did not hesitate in taking full advantage of David's worsening financial situation, viewing this as a business opportunity.

Nothing was working out for David and everyone seemed set against him. He felt that he had no option but to leave Brussels and try his luck somewhere else. He decided on Lisbon, Portugal. He begged Edzia to go with him to help him start a new life there. She blankly refused, as her loyalty lay with her mother above all else.

Edzia's heart did not soften towards her father; she continued to think of him as a difficult and dictatorial husband and father. She told herself that she would rather live in a garret and face a life of destitution than follow him to Portugal. However, she wanted to be married before his departure. And so it was to be.

Once more, the knitwear machines would be packed up and sent on ahead, this time to Lisbon.

Later on, she would regret her decision not to go with him. She admitted that she had been foolish, proud and misguided. Life could have turned out quite differently. She would have been spared the horror of the war, the Nazis and all of the suffering that she was to endure during that darkest of times. She even wondered if she might have been able to prevent her father's premature death. She would never know for sure. These questions and thoughts troubled her for the rest of her life.

Newly married

After her wedding and father's departure to Lisbon, Edzia began working for Kuba. His knitwear business was thriving. This became her sole source of income until the German invasion of Belgium in 1940. She worked long and hard hours. The newly-weds rented an unfurnished, two bedroomed basement flat which they shared with Chana, as well as some uninvited guests, mice and bugs! And very soon a little girl was born to Ilia and Edzia on 6th November 1936: Lydia Chapiro (my mother).

Eventually, Ilia and Edzia managed to save up enough money to partly furnish the flat. On returning home from work one evening, Edzia found that a bedroom suite, a cooker and some lamps had been installed. She learned that this was a late marriage gift from Kuba and Hela.

It was a constant battle fending off the mice and bugs. Edzia could never get rid of them. Seeing and hearing the mice scurrying around on the kitchen floor filled her with dread and fear. Reaching the limits of endurance, Edzia eventually placed a chair on top of the kitchen table and continued with her sewing there. Kuba had equipped her with a sewing machine so that she could work from home. At the time, this didn't seem a bad start to her married life. As time went on, Edzia would become the family's only breadwinner. Ilia eventually gave up being a travelling salesman and did not find other employment, leaving her no choice but to work like crazy to keep them going. She kept the wolves from the door and they survived!

When spring arrived, she suggested to Kuba that he purchase a machine that would enable her to make knitted swimwear. He agreed to buy the machine (using her salary) and soon his profits soared!

Edzia was completely dependent on Kuba for her financial subsistence. It was not until much later on (after the death of her father and the end of the war) that the full story of Kuba's schemes and plots against her father came to light.

However (before this) Hela and Kuba experienced a 'miraculous' change in fortune shortly after David's departure to Lisbon. They moved into a beautiful and spacious mansion house with servants. It was expensively furnished and equipped with all the latest comforts. Kuba installed his knitwear workshop in the basement of the house.

David Szklarz dies and a new life begins

David Szklarz died in 1936, less than a year after his arrival in Lisbon. He had continued to suffer from heart problems. His wife never got the chance to join him. Even so, they had grown so apart and estranged from one another that a happy reunion would have been an unlikely outcome. Edzia was unable to attend the funeral in Lisbon, as she was heavily pregnant with my mother at the time. She regretted this deeply. She was beginning to understand her father without prejudice or bias. A fuller and more accurate picture was emerging before her eyes and she began to feel the remorse which would plague her for the rest of her life. It was too late to make amends, to utter words of sorrow and regret.

However, life moves on. Shortly after her father's death, Lydia was born, assuaging the pain of Edzia's loss. She did not doubt, by then, that her father had loved her dearly. Edzia was 22 years old.

Rain in Lisbon, 1960 (Edzia narrates)

Years later, after the war, when Lydia had grown up and was living her own life in Israel, I decided to visit my father's grave in Lisbon. It was time for me to speak to him, to express my regret and sorrow, to let him know how foolish and mistaken I had been as a young woman.

Now I was re-married and had a new life in London. However, the ghosts of the past were never far, forever whispering in my ear.

The day I made my way to the Jewish Cemetery in Lisbon, it poured down. The sky was overcast with dark grey clouds. The heavens had opened and the rain fell steadily.

A taxi dropped me outside the gates of the cemetery on Av. Afonso. I carried a black umbrella with me. I had no idea where to start my search so I sought out the cemetery warden in his little office. I had already written my father's name on a piece of paper. I retrieved it from my pocket and unfolded the paper with icy, slightly trembling fingers, handing it to the janitor. He mouthed the words: DAVID SZKLARZ.

Then he opened a large, ancient- looking ledger and started scrolling down the lists of names, all handwritten in black, cursive script. He paused half- way down the page, marking the place with his finger. He gave me a knowing look and gestured me to follow him. We stepped outside into the rain. I opened up the black umbrella. The sound of the rain drummed noisily above my head and dripped all around me. There was a chill in the air.

We walked down narrow pathways, stepping over puddles, passing row upon row of tightly packed, identical-looking, horizontal tombstones, mottled with lichen and moss. As we meandered through the narrow lanes, my umbrella must have resembled a giant, shiny, black beetle scuttling across the cemetery.

Suddenly, the caretaker stopped in front of me. He pointed to a tombstone which looked like all the others in the cemetery. I stepped forward, trying to get a better look. I could just about make out the letters:

AV D Z L RZ

There was no doubting that this was my father's grave. The caretaker gestured, as if to say: 'It needs a good clean!' Then he walked away, leaving me in the middle of the cemetery.

The last time I had seen my father was in Brussels, 1936, before his departure to Portugal. I had been pregnant with Lydia, ignorant of how our lives would be turned upside down only a few short years later!

I remembered how confident I had been of my feelings at the time; how sure I had been of myself. I had not sided with my father and had no regrets in letting him go. I felt no sympathy for him. I believed I was right and never doubted myself for one moment. But I had been a proud and foolish young woman!

Now, so many years later, I had come to find him for the last time. What had I come for? I had almost forgotten. To ask for forgiveness, to tell him that I had misjudged him, to express remorse and regret, to make amends? To tell him about everything I had been through! But what I saw before me was not my father, David Szklarz, but a rain- splashed, cold slab of stone that had no meaning for me. I had nothing to say. I felt so cold. I found my way out of the cemetery, lit a cigarette and hailed a taxi. I returned to my hotel room with sodden shoes and wet hair, chilled to the bones.

The German Invasion & Occupation

The Second World War began in Europe when Germany invaded Poland on 1 September 1939. Although Britain and France declared war, nothing much happened on the western front, and Belgium and Holland remained neutral. It was not until May 1940 that Germany launched its *blitzkrieg* in the west, attacking Holland, Belgium and France. It was at this point that Edzia and her family decided to flee Belgium.

Edzia, Harry, Hela, Kuba, Ilia, Lydia (4 years old) and Chana together with some friends, planned to drive to the French border and cross over. The journey was difficult. The women and children travelled inside the car, whilst the men stood on the running boards, holding onto the doors, with the windows wound down. They travelled very slowly along the roads, following a convoy of refugees. Edzia did most of the driving. They would need to make many stops along the way, finding abandoned buildings to spend the night in. The children experienced the journey as an exciting adventure, staying in deserted houses every night which they would run up and down in and explore. Edzia took charge. She searched for coal and food supplies and organised everything along the way. Everyone relied on her. She was particularly concerned for Chana (who was diabetic) and Hela (who was very ill by this time). She took care of everyone and made them as comfortable as she could. The German army was advancing and isolated Stuka (dive- bomber) attacks were taking place upon the civilian population. The Luftwaffe was endeavouring to disrupt the movement of Allied troops by targeting civilian refugees in order to create chaos and panic.

One evening, they heard the sound of a plane overhead. Fearing for their lives, everyone made their way down to the basement of the abandoned house where they were staying overnight. Hela refused to move as she felt too ill and weak. Edzia stayed with her. She would not abandon her only sister to face the danger alone. Luckily, no bombing took place this time.

Towards the end of their journey, they ran out of petrol. Somehow, they made an arrangement with a farmer for the use of a horse which pulled the car for the last few miles. When they finally reached the French border, they were told that the Germans were already there. They had no choice but to turn back. The details of how they returned are not known to me.

The situation was developing at breakneck speed. Dark, ominous clouds were gathering and a deadly hurricane was about to be unleashed.

It was a time of chaos and confusion for the family, but the lens of time gives us a clearer picture of what was happening. Until May 1940 Belgium was still neutral and therefore British and French troops could not enter, even though Britain and France were pledged by treaty to defend the neutrality of Belgium. A German invasion was expected however, and detailed plans were in place to counter it. The Belgian army was to defend its frontier, using its modern forts, for three or four days, before falling back to a prepared line known as the KW/ Dyle line which ran from Antwerp, southeast to Namur, and then south to the French border. This would give time for the British Expeditionary Force (BEF) of about 250,000 men and 800,000 men of the French army to join the 600,000 men of the Belgian army on the line.

In practice, when the Germans invaded on 10th May, the frontier was breached in little more than a day. However, the defensive KW/ Dyle line was hastily established and held until 16th May. At that point it had become apparent that the Germans had broken through the lightly defended French line in the Sedan area on the French border, having come through Luxembourg and the southern Ardennes. This threatened to outflank the BEF and French army in Belgium. It was therefore decided to pull back to a line behind the Scheldt River, giving up Brussels and Antwerp. With 1.5 million allied troops on the move and about 1.5 million refugees on the roads, and attacks from Stuka dive bombers, there were giant traffic jams.

General Major Erwin Rommel commanded the 7th Panzer Division which was part of the force that came though the Ardennes. On 20th May he reached the sea at Abbeville on the Somme estuary in France, thus cutting off my family's attempted escape route. Incidentally, he had also cut off the BEF and the cream of the French army from their lines of supply with France.

On 23rd May the British commenced their retreat to Dunkirk. The Belgian army withdrew to a line behind the river Lys and the canal linking Ghent with the sea, effectively covering the retreat of the British and part of the French army. The Belgians held out for as long as possible, surrendering on 28th May.

The conquest of Belgium had taken just 18 days. The Netherlands had lasted 5 days under the same offensive. After the withdrawal from the KW/ Dlye line, Brussels had been declared an 'Open City', meaning that it was not defended. The Germans entered it on 17th May. On 1st June, Hitler flew in and had himself driven around the city.

When the Germans invaded Belgium in the First World War, they had committed atrocities against the civilian population. The allies made great use of this in their propaganda at the time. However, when the Germans invaded in May 1940 there were only isolated incidents of villagers being executed but, generally, they left the civilian population alone, and made an effort to present themselves in a humane and congenial light. However, this state of affairs was short-lived.

In 1940, Jews made up the largest non-Christian population of Belgium, numbering between 70-75, 000 out of a population of 8 million who were overwhelmingly Catholic. Most Jews lived in large towns and cities, such as Antwerp and Brussels. About half of the Jewish population (like Edzia's family) were recent migrants to Belgium fleeing anti- Semitism in Germany and Eastern Europe. Many of them were stateless refugees and only a small minority actually possessed Belgian citizenship. Secular Jews, like Edzia's family, tended to settle in Brussels, whereas more religious Jews settled in Antwerp.

After the completion of the German invasion, a military administration was established bringing the territory under the direct rule of the Wehrmacht (the unified armed forces of Nazi Germany). Within a few months, anti-Jewish legislation was enacted. Several pogroms took place in 1941, notably in Antwerp, and economic assets belonging to Jews were seized. From 1942, the occupation became much more repressive. Jews and Roma suffered systematic persecution and deportation, and there was much stricter repression of Belgian political dissent. In May 1942, Jews were forced to wear the Judenstern (Jew's Star) to mark them out in public.

To begin with, single Jewish males were called up by the German authorities to be sent away to work for the war effort. Many acquiesced, unaware that they were, in fact, being sent to concentration and death camps. However, it wasn't long before the Nazis started ramping up their activities by arresting people directly through the notorious round-ups and raids on Jewish communities and homes.

The Germans created a 'Judenrat' (an administrative body representing the Jewish community in German occupied territory). The AJB ('Association of Jews in Belgium') was formed and all Jews were required to register their details here. Using these registers, the Germans began deporting Jews to concentration and death camps in occupied Poland. Jews chosen from the lists were required to present themselves at a central collection point at the Dossin Barracks located in the city of Mechelen between Brussels and Antwerp. Those who ignored the order were arrested and taken to Mechelen directly.

Dossin Barracks (officially known as SS-Sammellager Mechelen/ SS Assembly Camp Mechelen) was set up as a detention/ transit camp to gather Belgian Jews and Roma ahead of their deportation to the extermination camps in Eastern Europe during the Holocaust.

The camp was established in March 1942 and was the only transit camp in Belgium. Formerly used as an army facility the site provided access to the railway freight dock. The three-storey block surrounded a large square courtyard (which could hold up to a 1,000 people) and was protected with barbed wire. It became operational in July 1942.

In 1942, approximately 90 percent of Belgium's Jewish population lived in the cities of Antwerp and Brussels. Mechelen was chosen as the site for the transit camp because its railway hub was situated halfway between the two cities.

The first group of people arrived in the camp from Antwerp on 27th July 1942. Between August and December 1942, two transports, each with about 1,000 Jews, left the camp every week for Auschwitz- Birkenau. Between 4th August 1942 and July 31st 1944, a total of 28 railway convoys left Mechelen for Poland, deporting over 25,000 Jews and around 350 Roma from Belgium to Eastern Europe. Most ended up in Auschwitz-Birkenau.

Rachel, a dear friend of Ilia & Edzia

Conditions at Mechelen transit camp were especially brutal. Rachel (a family friend) had borne witness to this during her forced internment there.

Rachel was one of the first to go. Like others, she believed that she was being sent away under forced labour to work for the German war effort. Before her departure, Edzia had supplied her with some extra provisions.

It was extremely difficult to get hold of extra food during this time. Because of the strict rationing in place, a black market in food and other consumer goods emerged. Food on the black market was extremely expensive. Prices could be 650 percent higher than in legal shops and rose constantly during the war. Because of the profits to be made, the black market spawned large and well- organised networks.

Edzia seemed to know her way around the black market and was able to acquire a regular supply of insulin for her mother (who needed injections three times a day due to her diabetic condition) as well as fish for Rosh Hashanah (the Jewish New Year)! Her Arian looks (copper-red hair, small pointed nose and sharp green eyes) gave her a better chance of escaping the notice of the Gestapo. She must have clutched her handbag tightly against her chest, hiding the yellow star sewn onto her coat.

*Compulsory wearing of the yellow badge in Belgium was enforced from May 27th 1942

Edzia sold what she could (on the black market) in order to keep the family going: jewellery, furs, ornaments, glass and silverware from the family's more prosperous days. The only articles she was able to save were her mother's diamond earrings, a silver drawstring evening bag, a set of finely engraved Russian wine glasses, a silver-topped crystal trinket jar, a gold watch and the silver candlesticks from Warsaw, Poland. All of these items remain with the family today.

Later on, Edzia learned what had happened to her good friend, Rachel. After some time in Mechelin, Rachel was placed in solitary confinement because she had become hysterical and was out of control. From there, she was transferred to a mental asylum in Duffel, Belgium, run by nuns. They saved her life by declaring her insane. They convinced the Germans that she was of no use to them and, consequently, she was left there.

Rachel remained under the care of the nuns until liberation in 1944. Once Ilia and Edzia knew of her internment there, they sent her regular food parcels every month. Rachel was not insane. However, spending the rest of the war in the company of mentally ill people had taken a terrible toll on her, which was only too apparent to Edzia and Ilia when they were finally reunited with her after the war. Ilia had gone to fetch her from the asylum and she stayed with Edzia and the family for two years in Brussels (she had no one else in the world) until she became well enough to be able to cope with everyday life. She found some secretarial work, rented a small flat and was able to live a normal life for some years in Brussels. She was a highly educated and cultured woman who had worked in a professional capacity before the war.

Rachel never spoke to Edzia about her experience in the camp. The only event she ever described was the following scene: the Commandant of the camp (SS Major Schmitt) frequently set his German Shepherd on the prisoners in the large square courtyard of the Mechelen transit camp to make them run faster during exercise drills. SS Major Schmitt ran the camp with brutal efficiency, maintaining order by use of extreme violence and terror in order to break the spirit of the prisoners. They were stripped of their identities; morally, emotionally and physically abused. The SS were given free rein to satisfy their sadistic and perverted impulses without consequence.

Tragically, Rachel eventually succumbed to despair and took her own life. She left her possessions to Edzia: a small brooch with tiny rubies, some books, a silk scarf and a little gold watch.

Dearest and beautiful Rachel

Hela

Soon after the death of David in 1936, Hela became ill. She was sent from clinic to clinic for various treatments but her condition did not improve. Kuba took advantage of her absences. Let's just say that his bed never remained cold for long and he enjoyed his pleasure with many women. Edzia's mother was no longer welcome in his home. She was in the way and he threw her out.

Hela was finally diagnosed with tuberculosis and spent a long period of time in a sanatorium. However, after several months, her condition seemed to deteriorate and a specialist was brought in who diagnosed Hodgkin lymphoma (an aggressive cancer that can quickly spread through the body). Edzia did not, initially, understand the seriousness of this condition which she had never heard of before. Hela was given one month to live. She died in Edzia's arms in 1941.

Alone

After losing her father and only sister, Edzia felt that she was left alone in the world. She would have to struggle for the survival of those in her family who still remained in that lovely country (Belgium) which she now called home and had grown so fond of.

How strange that she (the one who had always suffered from poor health and physical frailty) had survived to face the Holocaust. No one could have imagined such a thing.

The net closes in

> Between 1940 and 1942, anti-Jewish decrees were enforced. Firstly, all Jews had to be registered and counted. They were forbidden to work in the media or as civil servants, magistrates or teachers. Companies and businesses owned by Jews were identified and then either liquidated (sold) or 'aryanized' (confiscated and transferred to non-Jews). Forced labour was used. Children were excluded from the education system and the obligatory wearing of the Yellow Star was introduced. A curfew was imposed on Jews only.

Kuba had been able to procure two certificates: one for himself and the other for Ilia, which stated that they worked for a fur manufacturer who was supplying the German army with clothing for the Russian front (implying that they were essential workers for the German war effort). In reality, neither Kuba nor Ilia were employed in this way. However (if one had the means, which Kuba did) such documents could be purchased at a high price. A great deal of hope rested upon these permits to protect them from the clutches of the Nazis and deportation.

One afternoon, Edzia found herself alone at home. There was a pounding at the door. Two German soldiers entered the house. They ordered her to pack some belongings and go with them immediately. At first, she panicked and didn't know what to do. Then she remembered the certificate from Kuba! It was in her handbag and she handed it to them, explaining that only she and her husband lived in the house. They scrutinised the document very carefully. Edzia believed her heart stopped beating during those minutes and seconds. It was as if time itself stood still. Finally, they handed the papers back to her and ordered her to present herself to the German authorities with her husband, first thing in the morning.

As soon as they left, Edzia went into shock. She shook like a leaf and swallowed down a handful of aspirins in order to try and steady her nerves. She thought they might have closed off the street! This made her even more frantic as she imagined the worst: her mother and little Lydia in their clutches! She could bear it no longer and left the flat to search for them, full of apprehension and foreboding. Then she saw Chana and Lydia walking towards her and her heart almost burst with joy!

Edzia made up her mind then and there. Going to the Gestapo in the morning would be suicidal. They would be walking straight into the lion's den!

Ilia remains unconvinced

Even after this terrifying event, it would take Edzia all night to try and convince Ilia that the family must go underground without delay. Ilia did not believe that the Germans had malicious intentions. He remembered, with deep nostalgia, his experience as a prisoner of war during the First Word War, the Commandant's benevolence and the warm welcome he received from his kind wife. He recalled his wonderful experiences living in the beautiful city of Berlin in the 1920's. The German people were a nation of civilised, cultivated and honourable people.

They were not barbarians! Ilia refused to see what was unfolding before his eyes. Fond memories were clouding his judgement. But not Edzia. She remained clear- sighted, practical and realistic to the end.

In spite of everything, Ilia still had faith in the Germans. He insisted on speaking to the Commandant in person, believing that his perfect German, respect and admiration for Germany, its people and culture would impress the Commandant sufficiently to sway his opinion. There was no doubting that (in the light of this information) the occupying Germans would adopt a far more lenient and favourable attitude towards the family. Furthermore, he had his work permit! He did not, for one moment, believe they were in any danger.

There was no stopping Ilia. He made his way to the German authorities first thing in the morning, confident in the knowledge that once the Commandant heard the story of his youthful adventures, the misunderstanding would be cleared up in no time.

The hours passed by. Edzia waited anxiously but wasted no time in finishing her packing. At last, Ilia returned! They had let him go simply because, at that specific time, they were not arresting people classed as *apatride* (stateless). The German authorities were sticklers for petty officialdom and red tape. However, they had ordered him to return with his wife the following morning. Ilia realised (with crushing disillusionment) that his former connection with Germany made no difference, giving the family no advantage or protection whatsoever. There were no exceptions to the rule. The nostalgia which he had clung onto so desperately had blinded him from the stark and horrible reality unfolding before his eyes. At last, he agreed that they must flee. The wool was well and truly peeled away from his eyes now. Both he and Edzia had slipped through the net twice (miraculously) but their luck would surely run out a third time! The die had been rolled too many times already; this was not a time to dice with death!

Going underground

On the first day of Rosh Hashanah (the Jewish New Year), the family left their home on Rue Marie Christine with just a few suitcases. Rosh Hashanah would have been a festive time when friends and family would have gathered together for a special meal, anticipating the year ahead with optimism and hope whilst reflecting upon the year that had passed. Slices of apple would be dipped in honey, a loaf of soft, plaited challah bread sprinkled with poppy seeds would accompany a homemade meal with a selection of Chana's delicious, sweet pastries.

Some very dear and trusted Christian friends hid and shielded the family throughout the war. Edzia expressed a lifelong gratitude towards these cherished friends, Boris (of Russian descent) and Betty (originally from Switzerland). Like so many others, they put their own lives at risk in order to save their friends. Edzia kept the family going by gradually selling off bits and pieces of jewellery and silver. She bought provisions on the black market, paying exorbitantly high prices.

Kuba's tragic end

Shortly after Edzia's close encounter with the Gestapo, Kuba came to the conclusion that the false work permit he possessed did not guarantee protection from the escalating situation and inevitable deportation. It could no longer be relied upon. At this point, Harry was staying with Marie (Kuba's housekeeper) in the countryside.

Kuba had made up his mind that he would try and make his way to neutral Switzerland with Harry. He had procured false passports and was on his way to collect Harry, who was all packed and waiting for him, when he was arrested by the Germans. These were very dangerous times for Jews to be moving around in freely.

Kuba was deported to Bergen-Belsen concentration camp. He survived his imprisonment there. But, tragically, just before the end of the war, he died of typhus. Kuba and Hela's only son, Harry, was left orphaned by the end of the war.

> Bergen- Belsen was a Nazi concentration camp in northern Germany. From 1941 to 1945, almost 20,000 Soviet prisoners of war and a further 50,000 inmates died there. Outbreaks of typhus, tuberculosis, typhoid fever and dysentery occurred due to overcrowding, lack of food and poor sanitary conditions. Immediately before and after liberation (15th April, 1945), prisoners were dying at around 500 per day, mostly from typhus. This led to the deaths of more than 35,000 in the first few months of 1945. The British soldiers who liberated the camp discovered around 60,000 prisoners in the camp, most of them half- starved and acutely ill. They also discovered 13,000 unburied corpses. The BBC war correspondent, Richard Dimbleby, who accompanied the British troops, described the scene that greeted them:
>
> *...here over an acre of ground lay dead and dying people. You could not see which was which... The living lay with their heads against the corpses and around them moved the awful, ghostly procession of emaciated, aimless people, with nothing to do and with no hope of life, unable to move out of your way, unable to look at the terrible sights around them...*
>
> *This day at Belsen was the most horrible of my life.*
>
> 'Richard Dimbleby Describes Belsen' BBC News, April 15, 1945

After his father's disappearance, Harry remained with Marie for the remainder of the war. Edzia visited him several times (at enormous personal risk to herself). She found him to be contented, well fed and cared for. He had grown close to Marie who was warm and affectionate towards him. Edzia felt satisfied that she could leave him there for the rest of the war. Separating family members increased their chances of survival. Harry was as safe as he could ever be.

Kuba & David

The full extent of Kuba's disloyalty towards David only came to light after the war. From the first days in Poland, Kuba had already been hatching a plan to overthrow his father-in-law. It would seem that Kuba had harboured Machiavellian designs from the very start. He had not, for one moment, taken his eye off the prize: to be (at least) his father-in-law's equal in material success and wealth, whatever it took. According to Edzia, from the earliest days he embezzled funds from David's business and took advantage of his generosity. He had behaved deceitfully and dishonestly; he had been manipulative and scheming. By the time the family had re-located to Brussels, Kuba was (slowly but surely) stealing all business away from David. He was young, ambitious and determined. He had adapted more quickly and easily to his new circumstances, grasping every opportunity that came his way. David had needed to make several trips to London and Holland in order to chase money for unpaid invoices from various client orders. During this time, Kuba was left at the helm of the family business in Brussels and took full advantage of his father-in-law's absence, gaining the upper hand through double-dealing and swindling. David, faced with bankruptcy and financial ruin, left Brussels for the last time in 1936. He would never return. Kuba had outmanoeuvred and outdone his mentor and benefactor. He felt he owed David nothing and didn't give him one last glance back.

David Szklarz had weathered racial and economic persecution in both Russia and Poland, against the backdrop of 'The Great Depression of 1929- 39'. Kuba's machinations hammered the final nail in the coffin of his ruin. He was a beaten and exhausted man by the end.

A strange twist of fate

Edzia was very pained by all of this for the rest of her life. She and Ilia adopted Harry after the war, as he had been left orphaned.

Harry was, at first, reluctant to leave Marie (whom he had become very attached to during the war). It took a while to persuade him to live with Edzia and the rest of the family. A few seaside holidays helped to sway his opinion. It goes without saying that Edzia and Ilia treated him like a son (and more than that) to compensate for the tragic loss of his parents.

In procuring the false work permits, Kuba had saved Edzia from being arrested on that fateful day the Germans came knocking at the door. She owed him her life. And because of this, the family had a chance to escape the clutches of the Nazis and survive. Kuba was not so lucky. He had endured his terrible incarceration at Bergen- Belsen, only to lose his life shortly after the camp was liberated, leaving his only child, Harry, orphaned. The dramatic twists and turns of this story are heart- rending.

Survival and the knitwear machines

Edzia stood like a beacon in the fog. She held firm in the eye of the storm. She found inner reserves of strength and fortitude. Little Edzia, who had always been so sick and fragile. The world was spinning wildly out of control like a rabid, deranged beast, tearing at everything with salivating jaws and she stared right at it. They were trapped at the epicentre of a whirling vortex of total destruction, a lethal tornado smashing everything to smithereens. She would be tested to the very limits of her being. She bore the full weight of responsibility in keeping her family safe upon her very young and slight shoulders. She made all of the decisions and arrangements for them. One false move might cost them their lives. However, she turned out to be a force of nature, just like her father before her. She succeeded in protecting and saving them all, steadfast and unshakable in her resolve. Within that small frame, a lioness was in waiting, brave and fearless.

The knitwear machines had a life and story all of their own, like living things. They played their part in the drama and ever-changing fortunes of my family: travelling from Poland to Belgium and then to Lisbon, playing their part in men's fortunes and downfalls, changing hands and ownership, lying dormant and hidden during the war years. But their work was not done yet. They would re- enter the story after the war. They whirred, buzzed and clattered inside Edzia's ears, giving her no peace.

Lydia

My mother, Lydia, was born on 6th November 1936 at 168 Rue Marie Christine, Laeken, Brussels. She was the cherished and beloved only child of Ilia and Edzia Chapiro. There are many lovely pictures of her. And what a beautiful child she was, winning first prize in a baby beauty contest in 1938 at the age of two!

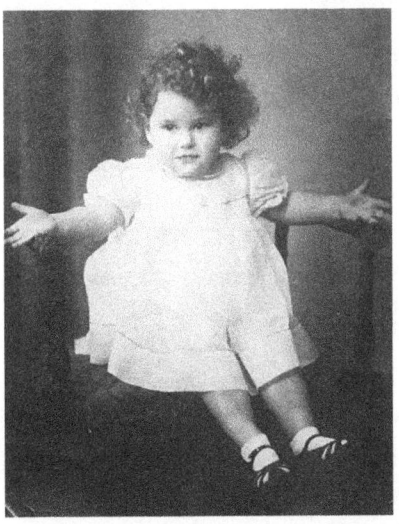

Lydia wins first prize! We can see why! What a beautiful child!

The photograph below was taken around 1939. Inga (the German Jewish girl standing on the far left of the image) was staying with my mother's family. But his would only be for a short period of time as it would not be long before Lydia and Harry went into hiding themselves. They would have been blissfully unaware of the sinister events unfolding around them.

From left to right: Inga, Lydia & Harry, Belgian coast,
just before the outbreak of war

First hiding place

By 1942, the round- ups and deportation of Jews was being ramped up by the Nazis. No one could deny (not even Ilia) that Jews were in mortal danger and that they were being sent to their deaths. The Holocaust was upon them and they had to find a way of saving the children.

Eventually, Edzia found a place for Lydia. She was placed in the home of a childless, middle- aged couple who lived in Jodoigne, (province of Walloon Brabant, Belgium) with four other little Jewish children. Lydia was around 6 years old by then. Edzia sent regular food parcels and paid the couple their fees by selling off her possessions, bit by bit. The payments increased each month by substantial amounts and Edzia was struggling to find the extra money.

After 3 months or so, Edzia travelled to see Lydia (at enormous personal risk to herself). She was shocked by what she discovered. Lydia had become so thin that Edzia could count every rib in her body, running her fingers down her ribcage like a xylophone. Lydia had always been a plump, chubby child. The couple had been keeping back the food parcels sent by parents, possibly selling on items and enjoying whatever was left over for themselves. It was evident that this couple were only interested in making money; they had no concern for the children's welfare. They were simply running a business and exploiting the situation to their own advantage.

Edzia did not hesitate in removing her child from the situation immediately and Lydia travelled back with her to Brussels. Better for her only child to take her chances with her own family than with strangers who did not care for her properly.

Looking back on this period, all Lydia remembered were freezing nights, hunger and fear. The children were left scared and alone in the dark. The couple prepared meals of porridge every day. In the morning the children would be served a watery porridge slop. At lunch time there was a porridge loaf which was cut into thin slices and sprinkled with salt and for dinner the children were offered the same porridge loaf but this time with sugar sprinkled on top. The children were ordered to remain quiet at all times and would often be sent out into the large garden to pick peas and beans for the couple in silence. One day, a little boy ran away.

> *'Je pense aujourd' hui que ma mère savait qu'un enfant sans amour est aussi un enfant mort...'*
>
> *'I think my mother understood that a child without love is a dead child...'*
>
> (From Lydia's testimony to honour René as one of 'The Righteous Among the Nations'- Yad Vashem ceremony, Brussels, 2000)

Second hiding place

Edzia was able to find a new place for Lydia through Madame Seghers, from Waterloo (one of David's old employees who had become a close and trusted friend of the family). Madame Seghers had recounted Lydia's story to a young man she knew by the name of René Ferier (aged 22), also from Waterloo. This young man had been so moved by the plight of this little girl and her family and so taken with her photograph that he decided then and there (with the agreement of his wife, Marguerite) to take Lydia into his care for the remainder of the war. After meeting Edzia and Ilia, a real feeling of trust was established and arrangements were made for Lydia to travel with René and his young family to Bioul, a small village in the Ardennes, where he managed a vast estate and chateau belonging to Le Baron Raymond Vaxelaire.

Edzia proposed a financial arrangement but René would not hear of it and refused any financial remuneration. He only asked that Edzia pay for new shoes, should Lydia require them. He also promised Edzia that (if the worst were to happen) she could rest assured that he would continue to take care of Lydia and bring her up as his own.

Edzia and Ilia would have René and his wife, Marguerite, to thank for Lydia's safety and happiness for the remainder of the war. 'Thanks' is a poor word to describe the depth of their lifelong gratitude. There was no doubting René's sincerity and intrinsic goodness from the very beginning. He was a man of quiet, unfaltering courage and resolution. He followed his principles, his values and beliefs. He would be risking not only his own security, but also that of his young family's by taking in a little Jewish girl. He never deliberated or hesitated over his decision. He followed his heart, what he felt and knew to be right. With the full support of his wife, Marguerite, my mother's life was saved. But more than that, she was always treated with great affection and consideration by the family. On the eve of Lydia's departure, Edzia needed to decide what she should pack for her only child. Clothes, shoes, some family photos and documents? She had no idea when she would see her little girl again. She experienced a profound feeling of gratitude but also grief and trepidation. She could not afford to dwell on her feelings, though, and swallowed down tears in total silence. She had to be strong. She was already exhausted.

Early Photographs of the Szklarz Family
(Russia & Poland)

Edzia- about two years old, probably taken in Russia around 1916

The Szklarz family: Chana, David, Hela & Edzia (the youngest)

Early image of Edzia and Hela with a toy lion, 1918

Edzia's Polish school ID card from Warsaw dated 1925/ 6- she was 11 or 12 years old in the photo

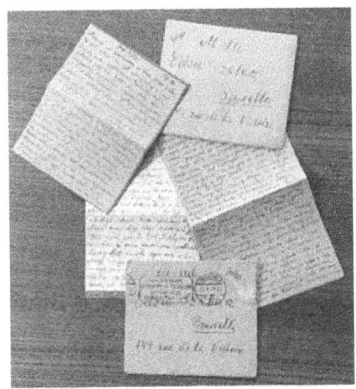 

Some letters written to Edzia in Polish from her friends in Warsaw and the front cover of her autograph book from Warsaw

Edzia and Hela with some friends in Poland, 1929. Edzia was fifteen years old in this image. A year later, the Szklarz family would relocate to Brussels, leaving everything behind them, never to return again

Edzia (holding a beautiful parasol), Poland, 1928

Edzia & Family in Belgium, 1930's onwards

Edzia and Ilia in Brussels, 1930's

Edzia on the Belgian coast before the outbreak of war

Edzia with Lydia who was born on 6th November 1936

Edzia and baby Lydia on the Belgian coast, 1936

Beautiful Lydia

Lydia (3 or 4 years old) and Edzia in Brussels

Hela and Kuba with little Harry

Harry

A tragic and sobering image of Kuba and Harry taken on the day of Hela's funeral. She was 32 years of age

The headstone reads:

> Helene Korn
> Nee Szklarz
> Varsovie
> 27- 10- 1909
> Bruxelles
> 16- 9- 1941

Note that this was during the occupation but before Jews were required to wear the yellow star.

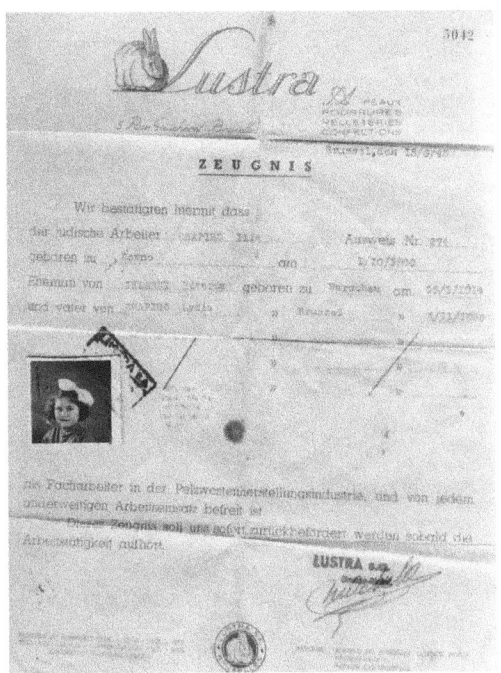

A very important document- a certificate dated 15/6/1943 (procured by Kuba), upon which rested the family's hopes to avoid arrest and deportation.

The document reads:

We confirm herewith that:

The Jewish worker <u>CHAPIRO Ilia</u>   Identification No. 274
Born in <u>Kovno</u>   on <u>1/10/1900</u>
Husband of <u>IKLARGE (Szklarz) Edwarda</u>   born in <u>Warsaw</u>   on <u>15/01/1914</u>

And father of <u>CHAPIRO Lydia</u>   born in <u>Brussels</u>   on <u>6/11/1936</u>

As a skilled worker in the production of fur jackets is exempt from any other work assignment/ posting.

This certificate permits us to retain his services in our employment with immediate effect up until such time as his employment is terminated.

Part 2 Lydia's Story

My mother spoke to me often about her war time experiences, so I will let her narrate her own story.

I was born at 168 Rue Marie Christine, Laeken, Brussels on 6th November 1936. By this time my parents had moved from their basement flat, leaving the mice behind for good!

Our family home was a first floor flat above a shoe shop. Let me describe it to you. My parents' bedroom was at the front, overlooking the street. Large double doors led from their bedroom to the dining room which had a big table and a fireplace which my father, Ilia, would light every morning. Folding doors with opaque glass panels led onto a small, in-between space. From here you went through into the lounge which was furnished simply with a sofa, some armchairs and a radio. This room was also used as a guest room and for Harry (my cousin) when my parents adopted him after the war. On a slightly raised landing there was a small kitchen. I remember blocks of ice being delivered up the stairs by 'icemen'. They filled our icebox in which we kept perishable foodstuffs such as cheese and milk. Next to the kitchen was an area with a large storage cupboard which led directly onto another room which I shared with my grandmother, Chana. And then lastly, at the very end of our bedroom, was a small toilet. This meant that every time someone needed to use the facilities, they would have to go through our bedroom. There was no bathroom. Basically, every room was interconnected, flowing into another room, like train carriages.

We washed ourselves using the kitchen sink. I remember how painful it was when Edzia tried to comb out the tangles in my thick, curly hair. She rinsed it in vinegar, saying it would make my hair strong and shiny. Ilia went to the Turkish baths regularly.

My grandmother Chana, who I called 'Bobonne', was in charge of the cooking. I must say, she was like a magician in that tiny kitchen. She practised alchemy with whatever ingredients she had to hand! Somehow, she was able to make chocolate during the war years. How she managed this, I could not tell you. What I can say, though, is that it tasted wonderful and I remember it to this day. A tin of sardines could be transformed into a delicious meal! She was inventive and resourceful. The storage cupboard was full of tins, butter, flour, sugar, eggs and other provisions. This was Chana's domain.

I disliked sharing a room with my grandmother as a child. She slept on a large, raised bed and I on a much lower, smaller one. Chana's bed was covered in big, plumped up feather pillows and a heavy Polish eiderdown. As she slept and snored, I imagined a great whale under the heavy quilt which rose up and down with every whistle and grumble. I felt far away from my parents who slept in a bedroom at the other end of the flat.

I made my own private play area in the small space between the dining room and lounge. If I closed both sets of folding doors, I could shut myself away from everyone. I played in this private space with my dolls for hours on end by myself. I don't remember anyone playing with me (my mother was always working, my father either reading the newspaper or napping and my grandmother was simply too old and ill-tempered). I know Chana took me to the park. But she seemed very old to me and just sat on the bench. We couldn't communicate easily, as she didn't speak French and I knew no Yiddish or Polish. My parents had decided that my first language would be French. However, they often spoke to one another in Yiddish. To my very young eyes, my grandmother was ill-humoured and stern. I do not remember her being affectionate towards me, although I am sure that she loved me. Of course, I was not aware of the impact her illness (diabetes) may have had on her general wellbeing and moods.

I remember being reminded constantly by my mother, Edzia, to always be respectful and considerate towards my grandmother.

I should not make noise whilst grandma rested. So, I played very quietly, trying not to disturb Chana or displease my mother.

A good child and Titine

I suffered from a lack of privacy and I felt my little life to be quite restricted. I always had to consider other people's wishes, comfort and needs before my own. I think I was a very obedient child and did what I was told. I never caused a fuss. Friends could come and play, from time to time, but only if Chana was consulted first and agreed.

As a baby, I was sometimes looked after by Titine, one of David Szklarz's, old employees, who had become a good friend of Edzia's. I never met my grandfather, David Szklarz, as he died in Lisbon, Portugal, the year of my birth. Below is a cute photograph of me with Titine.

Baby Lydia, in the arms
of Titine, Brussels, 1936

Dolls and the cellar

I had two very large and beautiful dolls, taller than myself! I believe these dolls were stored in the cellar when we were getting ready to leave our flat to go into hiding. Many things got lost during that time, of course.

But my favourite doll, the one that I carried with me everywhere, was a very ordinary rag doll with a missing limb. I wrapped her up in a blanket and would not be parted from her. I think she must have travelled with me to Bioul, when I went into hiding with the Ferier family later on in the war, during the German occupation of Belgium.

The cellar under our house really filled me with terror as a young child. This is where we stored the coal. To me, the cellar was a dreadful black hole and I feared something horrible might come for me from its dark depths. It was the stuff of nightmares and I avoided going there!

> During the German occupation, Lydia was put into hiding a second time with the Ferier family. As you will remember, her first experience had been disastrous and Edzia had wasted no time in retrieving her from the couple who had been looking after her, as soon as she realised how poorly the children under their care were being treated.

Bioul

On arriving in Bioul as a six year old child, I was introduced to the residents of the village as a cousin from Brussels: Lydia Chapirotte. They were informed that my family had decided it would be beneficial for my health to take in the air of the Ardennes and to experience the calm of the countryside, as opposed to life in a hectic city, where it was impossible for a child to thrive. The only members of the community who knew about my true identity were

Dr Crespeigne, the mayor, the manager of the quarry and the village priest. René carefully hid my identity papers behind some bricks in the bedroom wall which I shared with Suzy, René and Marguerite's young daughter, who was about two or three years old at the time. He papered and painted over the secret hiding place.

From the very beginning, I was welcomed into the very heart of this loving family who always showed such kindness and concern for me. I remember playing with the other children in the village square and attending the local school which was just opposite our house. I never experienced hunger and had happy, warm memories. It would not be an exaggeration to say that I was able (not just to survive) but to flourish there.

The Ferier's lived in a large, stone house which stood on a corner plot in the centre of the village. The rooms were spacious and there was a garden. The entrance to the chateau was accessed from the village itself. Beyond the wrought iron gates and stone walls was the promise of something quite magnificent and enchanting.

Le Baron Raymond Vaxelaire had vacated the estate for the remainder of the war. René was the estate manager, in effect, with numerous and important responsibilities and duties. He had to oversee and was in charge of hundreds of hectares of forest and farmland, tenants, stable yards, kitchen gardens and orchards, horses and cattle, the beautiful chateau with its chapel and grounds, including landscaped gardens, a lake and a vast park. There was an army of staff to supervise and organise: gardeners, gamekeepers, wardens, rangers, stewards, farmers, housekeepers, stonemasons and stable hands.

The church

The village school was run by the nuns. I received a Catholic education and attended church every Sunday. The church made a deep impression on me. I found it truly dazzling! Everyone was so welcoming and generous. To this day I remember how wonderful and beautiful it was to my eyes: the arrangement of fresh flowers in vases, golden artefacts glinting in the light, gilt framed paintings of saints, ornate carvings, statues of the Madonna and child, brass candlesticks, stained glass windows depicting religious scenes, strong colours, arresting religious iconography, the scent of incense and polish, the hushed echoing of prayers and hymns. I was drawn to the ambience of solemnity. As a reward for being good, I was allowed to arrange the flowers for Sunday mass on a few occasions. I watched (in awe) as other children took their first communion. The girls dressed in their long, white dresses and lace veils filled me with longing. I hoped and prayed that I too would, one day, be lucky enough to walk down the aisle in such a dress! If only the war would last just long enough for this to happen! The sacred chalice sat upon the altar which was covered in a crisp, white linen cloth which had a magnificent cross embroidered in gold, silver and red thread. I longed to taste the consecrated wine and bread to truly be part of this experience!

I remember this prayer:

> Je vous salue Marie,
> Pleine de grace,
> Le seigneur est avec nous,
> Maintenant et à l'heure de notre mort,
> Ainsi soit- il...

There was a private pew for the Vaxelaire family in the chapel. Every Sunday I hoped to catch a glimpse of the noble and aristocratic Baron. But he never appeared. However, I did not dwell on these thoughts for long, as I found myself busy with everyday family life, the church, school and being René's little companion.

Adventures with René

Suzy was too young to accompany her father on his various errands around the estate. However, he took me with him, perched *on the handlebars of his bicycle as he made his rounds. I remember we visited farms where René purchased supplies and provisions. He introduced me to all sorts of people working on the estate as 'Our little cousin from Brussels'. And that was, indeed, how I felt from the very beginning: a sense of place and belonging within the warm embrace of the Feriers. I participated in every outing, festivity and celebration as a member of the family. René was, undoubtedly, a father figure in my eyes. I felt protected and loved by him. I grew to treasure him like a second father.*

René was always careful to respect my Jewish roots and heritage. However, I became increasingly drawn to the customs of a Catholic upbringing. I was happy to observe all of the Catholic religious rites. This gave me a profound sense of belonging but, also, prevented suspicion from being aroused.

Christmas

Christmas was a lovely time. Real candles decorated the branches of an enormous Christmas tree in the middle of the village square. When the candles were lit on Christmas Eve, I don't think I had seen anything quite as beautiful. Suzy and I would help Marguerite decorate our own tree inside the house and it felt magical. After Midnight Mass, the priest would organise a meal for all the villagers in a barn which was wonderfully decorated with holly, ivy and mistletoe. There were long benches for us to sit on and oak refectory tables laden with black pudding, steaming mashed potatoes and hot apple compote. To this day, I love this meal. It brings me a feeling of deep comfort, warmth and happiness. I am transported back to Bioul on Christmas Eve.

Marguerite always prepared a wonderful meal on Christmas day and for dessert there was chocolate mousse! Marguerite let me gorge on it until I was sick! It was Christmas, after all! Suzy and I received homemade Christmas gifts: knitted animals, scarves and hats from Marguerite and toys carved out of wood from René.

Happy memories

Food was plentiful in Bioul. There was butter and chocolate, meat, vegetables, freshly baked bread, cheese and eggs, homemade preserves, apples, pears and cherries. Most of the produce was grown on the estate itself. We were not affected by food rationing or shortages. I wonder how my parents managed in Brussels during this time? I know Edzia (my mother) sold off many of her possessions to see them through the war years. She bought most of their provisions on the black market.

René was a homely man who enjoyed family life. He cooked, made bread, cured his own ham and distilled his own alcohol in the cellar using apples from the local orchards and farms. I will always remember the sweet smell of fermenting apples pervading through the house. Unlike my own father, René was always busy and active. He made repairs around the house and involved himself with the upbringing of the children. He played with us and took us for walks around the estate and surrounding countryside. He allowed us to run around the grounds of the chateau under his supervision and play in the fountain on hot summer days.

Suzy and Lydia in the grounds of the chateau on
a summer's day and enjoying a splash in the fountain

School and the nuns

As mentioned before, the village school I attended was run by the nuns. At first, they seemed like strange, black, flightless birds to me in their long dark gowns which flapped like wings as they passed by. In fact, they reminded me of crows. I wondered, secretly, if there was any hair underneath their habits. Or were they completely bald? The nuns were severe in both demeanour and expression. A strange smell hovered around them like a cloud: a blend of something sour, acrid and musty.

At the front of the classroom was a big blackboard covered in eye-catching, vivid drawings. Using coloured chalks, the nuns depicted scenes from the New Testament and illustrated the crucifixion of Christ. Chalk dust remained on their fingers and stained their black robes. I was utterly fascinated by these powdery, chalky images in strong colours. The nuns explained to us that Jesus' wounds had been dabbed with vinegar. This image disturbed and fascinated me for a long time and the smell of vinegar always brought it back to me.

At first, I felt a little intimidated by the nuns. But I soon grew accustomed to them as they became familiar figures within the landscape of my new life in Bioul. They taught me how to read and write and I learned the catechism.

Butter

One day, Marguerite sent me on an errand to collect some butter from a local farm. By then, I was known to all of the villagers who always greeted me so nicely. I felt confident enough to go alone, familiar with the route. As I was walking down the country lane, I thought I saw some German soldiers in the distance coming towards me in a car. I stopped dead in my tracks and became paralysed with fear. I turned back and arrived home without the butter, feeling ashamed and guilty. Although Marguerite was a little displeased, I remember René saying: 'We'll go together'. And off we went to collect the butter.

Looking back on that incident, I cannot really say whether there had been German soldiers or whether it was my imagination. All the same, it shows that fear was alive in my heart.

Edzia's Visit

Edzia could not visit Lydia often from Brussels, where she was trying to keep herself and the rest of the family hidden and safe. Travelling was difficult due to the disruption of transport during those times of upheaval and chaos; it would have been extremely dangerous for a Jewish person, exposing them to arrest and deportation.

Edzia procured a false identity card for her visits to Bioul. She was 'Madame Dupont', in case she was stopped by the Germans. She counted on her Arian looks to avoid their clutches. Still, it took an enormous amount of courage as the risks were high. Whilst making her way to see Lydia, she would repeat the name 'Madame Dupont' over and over in her head (lest she forget) as you never knew when there would be random checks or round-ups. Her heart raced like mad.

Edzia reached Bioul by any means she could, sometimes arriving with a horse and cart, sitting on a bale of hay. Her stays had to be short. She needed to return to the city before curfew and the fall of darkness. She had to get back to her ailing mother and Ilia, who both depended on her.

She recalled the end of one visit when it was time for her to leave. She asked Lydia to be a good girl and go upstairs to prepare for bed. She would come up to say goodnight soon, after she had spoken with René and Marguerite. After a while, Edzia climbed the stairs, her heart pounding, fearing the pain of their imminent separation. She opened the bedroom door, made her way to the bed and sat on the edge. Lydia said it was cold in the bed. So, Edzia got under the covers with her. Suddenly,

Lydia flung her arms so tightly around her neck, almost strangling her. Edzia could hardly breathe. The embrace was so strong and Lydia would not let go. She was in floods of tears, sobbing her heart out. She pleaded for Edzia not to leave her and to take her home. She wanted to be with her, papa and sufta (grandma)! Edzia promised her that very soon, they would all be together again. She prized her arms away, tucked her under the bedcovers and kissed her goodnight. She promised she would not leave her bedside until she was fast asleep. After a little while, Edzia got up and made her way to the bedroom door, closing it quietly behind her with trembling hands. She could barely make her way downstairs (her legs had turned to jelly) as she clutched the banister tightly for support. She embraced René and Marguerite and thanked them with all her heart in a broken voice before saying her farewells and departing.

She was sure of only one thing at that point in time: that her daughter was as safe and well cared for as she could possibly hope for. She could not say, however, with any certainty, what the future had in store for any one of them. This was a terrible time, but she had to remain strong and hopeful.

When she returned to Brussels, she hid Madame Dupont's identity card, as she would surely need to use it again.

This is how Lydia remembered that day

One day, René and Marguerite told me that Edzia was coming to visit me. I waited expectantly by the window for my mother's arrival. My heart was bursting with excitement. I waited and waited. The day seemed to go on forever. But still she did not come. As the hours passed and the bright day gradually turned dark, grey and cloudy, despair seeped into my heart.

At long last, very late in the day, Edzia finally arrived. She was dropped off by a horse and cart. I was warned that her visit would be short. I longed for her to stay with me that night but I also knew that this was out of the question.

We spent a little bit of time together before she told me that I needed to get ready for bed. But she promised me that she would remain with me until I fell asleep. I remember not wanting to cause my mother any trouble (understanding that she had to travel back). I pretended to fall asleep so that she could leave. I heard the bedroom door close softly and then her footsteps descend the staircase. This is all I remember.

> What strikes me about these two accounts is how different they are. Lydia did not describe this meeting in the same way as Edzia remembered it. My feeling is that the little child buried her painful emotions so as not to upset her mother and that Edzia (my grandmother) was a woman of enormous strength and courage.

More about René

Whilst taking care of a little Jewish girl, René was also helping the Belgian resistance. Arms were concealed in the chapel and some of the fighters were hidden in the chateau itself. He supplied them with food and provisions throughout the war, once again, at great personal risk to himself and his family. René was a highly principled man. He made decisions based upon his values and moral judgement. He never equivocated and was resolute in his beliefs and actions. He told no one about the above until many years after the war.

Courage is an over- used word, perhaps. How can I begin to explain the qualities René possessed? He was a man of integrity and unwavering commitment to what he instinctively knew to be right. Certainly, he was a man of principle, and yet so much more than that. He was steadfast and reliable. I felt completely safe under his care. I felt that as long as René was with me, nothing bad could happen. And yes, he was brave but more importantly, he was a kind and loving human being who followed his heart.

In spite of the German occupation of Belgium, I was able to live a normal and carefree childhood, whilst nestled within the protective and affectionate arms of the Ferier family in Bioul.

The young René Ferier with the
Christmas tree in the background

A visit in the night

One evening, René was visited by a high-ranking German officer at the house in Bioul. Representing the Baron in his absence, Rene was the first to be called upon by the Commandant. The officer was making enquiries about the estate and René's position. He may also have been looking for hidden Jews, resistance fighters and weapons. He enquired as to who lived in the house and asked to search it with his men. René permitted them access. However, when the German officer started to make his way upstairs, René stood directly in front of our bedroom door, preventing him from entering. He informed the officer that he forbade his men to enter the room where his children were sleeping. The officer did not insist and moved on to check the rest of the upstairs rooms and attic.

No doubt, René also took the officer on a tour of the chateau and its grounds, as the Germans were considering requisitioning the chateau for their own use. By morning, there was no sign of the officer or his squad. They had vanished into air.

Only after the war was this story related to me. I realised then, that a simple wooden door and René's presence of mind had shielded me and saved us all from a tragic fate.

Embroidered flags

The nuns of my school had spent the war years embroidering flags for each of the allies. Finally, the day came when talk of Liberation filled the air like firecrackers! A lookout was stationed on the road to inform the village of any developments. Suddenly, we saw the lookout running towards the village, waving his arms above his head and shouting that the Americans were approaching! The nuns immediately unravelled their beautifully embroidered allied flags and hung them out. We children had climbed up to the attic to watch events as they unfolded before us. No sooner had the nuns hung out their hand sewn bunting, than the lookout returned (running like the wind) and barely catching his breath, he announced, 'No, the Americans are not coming! It's the Germans!' As quickly as they could, the nuns gathered in the flags and all of the villagers returned to their houses, bolting the doors behind them. Indeed, not long after this, we witnessed a defeated German army retreating and on the run! They passed through our village, desperate looking soldiers, grabbing bicycles and carts to carry their wounded in. German trucks and jeeps whizzed through the heart of the village. It seemed to go on for hours before there was a sudden lull. Then the running feet of our trusted lookout were heard once again and this time he announced, 'Now the Americans are coming!'

The nuns quickly unwound the flags and hung them out once again. Everyone came out of their houses and lined the street with bated breath. There was absolute silence. Everyone's heart was in their mouth! We children still watched from the attic. And then, in the distance, we heard and saw them approaching. Steadily, calmly and confidently, American troops entered Bioul. They were here, at last! It was unbelievable!

> This would have been in early September 1944 when most of Belgium was liberated quickly, although pockets of German resistance held out until February 1945.

Americans and white bread

I had never seen Americans before. To my child's eyes the soldiers towered above us: tall, strong and healthy. They smiled at us with beautiful, perfect, gleaming white teeth. Their uniforms looked so smart and clean. Their jeeps and trucks were new and shiny. This was in sharp contrast to the British soldiers we had seen who looked ashen faced and malnourished and whose threadbare uniforms hung on their thin frames. They had been fighting for a long time and looked so weary in comparison to the fresh-faced young Americans who descended on Bioul.

After speaking to René, the American Major gave the order for a big tent to be set up in the very centre of the village square. We children watched with fascination as they erected, before our wide and incredulous eyes, a fully functioning bakery. They wasted no time in churning out loaves of freshly baked white bread. The first batch was distributed amongst the children of the village. They gave us chewing gum and chocolate. We thought they were gods and that we were in heaven!

The young American Major was invited for dinner and René introduced him to the family. He explained that I was a Jewish child whom he and Marguerite had been hiding during the war.

The Major was very moved by my story, he was Jewish himself. He did not hesitate in telling René that if my parents had not survived the war then he would come back for me and take me to America with him to be brought up with his Jewish family. As you know, René had already made a promise to Edzia that he and Marguerite would continue to take care of me under these circumstances. So, I don't know what he said to the American Major.

However, what I do know is that the Major was killed by the Germans two days later. The fighting was not over yet.

And that is why, for me, liberation started with a loaf of freshly baked white bread, chewing gum and chocolate.

VE Day

After liberation, at the age of nine, I returned home to my parents and grandmother (all of whom had survived the horrors of the war) at 168 Rue Marie Christine. I was very ill with gastroenteritis and had a very high temperature. However, I remember so clearly, my mother entering my bedroom and declaring that I had to get up and go out onto the street to see the celebrations taking place for VE Day (the end of the war in Europe). I could barely move, let alone stand up. I felt so weak and sick and was suffering from severe abdominal spasms. She wouldn't take no for an answer, though. She helped me up, threw a blanket around my shoulders and supported me as we made our way down into the street which was jam packed. My head was spinning. There was mayhem everywhere. We could hardly move through the throngs of people who shouted, sang and laughed all at the same time. The crowds pushed and heaved. We were being swept along by this human tidal wave, almost crushed! The atmosphere pulsated with heightened intensity and excitement, chaos and hysteria. Celebration, jubilation and elation ran through the streets of Brussels like an electric current. The crowds were going mad!

Suddenly, someone shouted, ' V-1!' Everyone stopped dead in their tracks and looked up at the blue sky. There was absolute silence. Elation turned to fear at the spin of a coin. There was so much talk at the time about the V-1, also known as the Buzz Bomb, the Doodlebug or the Kirschkern (cherrystone). No one moved. No one dared to breathe. All eyes were turned upwards. A false alarm. The crowds took up their wild cheering once again.

Edzia would not let me miss this sight. It marked the end of our struggle for survival, the end to the horror of war and our persecution. I felt that I was going to faint. I could barely keep myself steady and upright. I felt as sick as a dog. The scenes in front of me swam before my eyes like a mirage. I have never forgotten that day, and always remember it alongside Inga's tragic death.

Survivors and fabulous meals

After the war, my parents searched for anyone known to them who had survived and my father brought them back to Rue Marie Christine. There were few. However, whoever stepped over the threshold of our door would be fed and offered a roof over their heads for as long as they needed it.

Rachel stayed with us for two years. Lily Goldberg, whose parents had perished in a concentration camp, lived with us for some time also. She was only 16 years old and was the sole survivor in her family. What I remember about her were the wooden clogs she wore on her feet when she first arrived at our home. These wooden clogs came from the concentration camp she had been held in.

And then there was Harry, my cousin. After much convincing and some holidays by the seaside, Harry finally agreed to come and live with us. Harry was a teenager by then and a difficult boy. He was full of anger, understandably. He had a strong personality, like Edzia, and they clashed on many occasions. There were many scenes between them, involving shouting and arguments. I tried to close myself off from it all in the little play area I had created for myself between the dining room and lounge. I found it distressing to bear witness to their raised tempers. My mother was exhausted. She worked tirelessly to make ends meet: sewing and making hosiery items from the knitwear machines retrieved after the end of the war. I felt I had to tiptoe around her. I couldn't bear the thought of causing her anguish or upset because I knew she had kept us all safe and alive! Harry never held back. There were tantrums and outbursts. I thought my mother might shatter into a thousand pieces of splintered glass. It terrified me when I saw this escalation in anger. I thought the world would cave in on us. I shied away from it all and made myself invisible.

My family was not religious. However, there would always be gatherings on festive days like Rosh Hashanah, Hanukkah and Passover. Chana liked to preserve the traditions and she particularly enjoyed cooking on these occasions.

I think my parents held these gatherings more for the children's sake (Harry and I). So many had perished in the war; it was important to bring those that had survived together. These were gatherings meant for close friends and family; there was no religious observance.

Chana, with my mother's help, would be busy in the kitchen for days in advance preparing delicious typical Ashkenazi food. Many wonderful dishes and aromas came out of that small kitchen. The silver candlesticks, which Edzia had managed to save, always accompanied these special meals, alongside silver cutlery and the finely engraved, delicate wine glasses (astonishing that they had survived the war!). The candlesticks were given an extra polish on these occasions, which made them catch the soft light in a particularly beautiful way when the candles were lit.

For Pesach/ Passover, I remember a feast of dishes and numerous courses: lokshen soup with kneidlach and kreplach, gefilte fish with horseradish, matzos, roast chicken with potatoes, sweet carrots and peas, stewed prunes and apricots and the famous almond cake with chocolate mousse. Chana would make matzo brei for us in the mornings. On other days we enjoyed latkes, klops (meatloaf with a hard- boiled egg in the middle), schnitzel, chopped liver, plaited loaves of soft white challah sprinkled with sesame or poppy seeds and freshly baked bagels. Leftover pieces of challah would be dipped in milk and egg and then fried for me and Harry to enjoy. On Fridays, Chana would prepare a wonderful cholent: a big pot filled with brisket of beef, potatoes, beans and barley was left to cook slowly overnight in the oven on a low heat ready for lunch on Shabbat. Warm, deep aromas filled our home and made our mouths water in anticipation. Many gloriously sweet desserts, cakes and pastries emerged from the tiny kitchen, especially around the time of Rosh Hashanah. My grandmother, Chana, was the queen of all things sweet and delectable: rugelach, honey cake, blintzes filled with soft cheese, sweet lokshen kugel, apple kuchen, poppy seed cake, chocolate babka, chewy macaroons and, of course, the almond cake with chocolate mousse! The taste of chocolate mousse would always bring me back to Christmas time in the little village of Bioul.

Cherries in brown paper bags

My father, Ilia, was a passive and docile man. After the war, I accompanied him (every single morning) to the offices of various Jewish Agencies that printed out lists of survivors. Hundreds of people flocked there, scouring the names from top to bottom, desperately searching for someone they knew. Ilia did the same, with me in tow. He found Lily this way and brought her home to us.

Ilia would also take me to Le Gare du Nord every day. I remember the fruit stalls in the station where Ilia always stopped to buy a bag of shiny, red cherries. We sat on a bench for hours on end, watching the trains arrive. I remember the survivors disembarking, clothed in their concentration camp striped uniforms and wooden clogs. They had grey, old faces. Their eyes were sunken and hollow, void of expression or furtive and desperate looking. It was difficult to distinguish men from women, young from old. As they stepped onto the platform, Ilia offered them cherries out of brown paper bags.

I have often wondered why my father spent so much time watching the survivors arriving at the station every day. Did he feel a sense of guilt at having survived? Did he regret not being part of the resistance?

I will never know for sure. I never asked him. We watched the scenes at the train station in silence and I have never forgotten those bright red cherries in their brown paper bags.

Then on leaving he would say to me, 'Never forget.'

Not once did Edzia accompany us. She was far too busy working to put food on the table, taking care of Chana and the survivors under our roof.

Still wanting to go to Sunday Mass and seaside holidays with the Ferier family

After the war (9 years old and with the memories of the church and my Catholic experience still fresh in my mind) I announced to my mother that I wanted to die so that I could go up to heaven! I insisted that I wanted to carry on attending Sunday Mass. She did not oppose this wish. However, I overslept on the first Sunday. Edzia said, 'Never mind. You can go next week.' But the following Sunday, I overslept yet again! And this continued until, eventually, the desire faded away and was forgotten. Life started to take on a new shape and direction for me.

Today, I wonder if I was so drawn and attracted to Catholicism as a child because I had been brought up in a secular household. For a time, I desired to cling onto it and the promise of a better life beyond. An abstract and tantalising concept that very much appealed to me, I think.

After the war, I spent many a lovely summer holiday by the seaside on the Belgian coast with the Ferier family. They did not forget me and created more happy memories for me.

Holidaying with the Ferier family for many years after the war. Lydia is in the middle

Harry

Harry and I grew up together like a sister and brother. We had always been very close and we loved one another very deeply. When Harry moved in with us after the war, he was around the age of 14, I think, about 5 years older than me. He was legally adopted by Edzia and Ilia shortly after. I looked up to Harry, I trusted him, followed him and believed in him. He looked after me and protected me. I thought my parents gave him privileges which I did not enjoy, but I always forgave him for it.

When Harry turned 15, Edzia and Ilia organised a late Bar Mitzvah for him at home (the initiation ceremony of a Jewish boy who has reached the age of 13). This was meant as a deeply symbolic gesture with a profound meaning. There were no prayers or sermons, no readings from the Torah (as is usual). Instead,

Harry read out a deeply moving speech, in remembrance of his lost parents and all those who had perished in the Holocaust.

Close family friends came. There was a homemade meal and singing led by a cantor.

I remember deliberating for hours over which skirt to wear for the occasion? They were both made out of a pretty cotton print with tiny flowers. However, one was yellow and one was pink. So, which was it to be? I'm afraid I can't tell you because I don't remember!

An orange from the land of Israel

One day, we had a visit from Chanan, a relative who had fought with the Jewish Brigade of the British army during the latter part of the war. Chanan lived in Israel. When he came to visit us after the war at Rue Marie Christine, he took out an orange from his knapsack which came all the way from his kibbutz. To me, he was like a magician, making an orange appear like a rabbit out of a hat! He had kept that orange during all those months of fighting. He had saved it for us. Yes, it was a little desiccated and wizened. But it represented something far larger, far greater. The tantalising possibility of a new and different kind of life, a new dawn. After his visit, I kept the orange on my bedside table so that I could contemplate it every evening in solitude. It hinted at the promise of something else, beyond the shadows and darkness of the war we were emerging from.

Une crise de nerfs

I had seen my mother Edzia (after the war) attacked by 'une crise de nerfs' on several occasions. In English, you would call it a nervous breakdown. In the eyes of a child, it was frightening to behold. She shook uncontrollably, she cried and shouted. She lost control. It was violent. I can hardly find the words to describe what I witnessed as a child and I cannot forget those scenes.

Perhaps it seemed worse than it actually was. But I don't think so. It filled me with anxiety and dread and has left an indelible mark on my memory.

On one occasion, it had been something Harry said that had provoked her into this state. I felt utterly torn between the two of them, loving them both so intensely. I became mute, paralysed with fear, believing that the whole world would come crashing down around us. I wished to disappear, like a magician, upon closing the glass partition doors around my private play area between the two rooms.

I did everything I could to avoid such a scene from occurring. I tried to make life as easy as possible for Edzia. I didn't want to burden her with anything. I kept all of my feelings 'hidden'. I felt it was my duty to protect her. She had been through so much and had saved us.

I had been a hidden child during the war and somehow, it carried on after the war too. It was never resolved. I concealed all of my emotions from my mother and I continued to carry that hidden child within me. I was never free, never unburdened. There was a barrier between us and we were never able to talk about things openly. I kept this inner child invisible and safe. I could not trouble my mother with her. I was careful to keep her in check at all times. She was never released, but could not be forgotten either. I felt that I should just be grateful to be alive.

I had lived in my mother's shadow as a child. The story of the war was hers. She was the main protagonist. She had saved us all and was a heroine in our eyes. A most remarkable woman. I knew that I owed her my life. I did not feel that I was entitled to my own individual feelings. Such thoughts filled me with guilt. I felt so small and insignificant compared to her and all she had done. She had been so strong, magnificent and brave. Her character and personality seemed to dominate everything. I would need to find some space for myself so that I could grow into a woman too in order to live my own life, have my own story and place in the world.

As an adult, I have often asked myself the question: would I have acted in the same way as Edzia? Would I have tried to save my child at any cost, meaning placing her in the hands of complete strangers?

There is no doubt in my mind that I could not have found myself in a better place than with the Ferier family in Bioul. They saved me with affection and love in their hearts. I was lucky. Nevertheless, it puzzles me (to this day) that I only seem to have retained happy, warm memories from that time. Surely, a six- year- old child would have struggled with other, less palatable feelings?

Early post war memories of my parents, Edzia and Ilia

After the war, Edzia never stopped working. I didn't get to spend much time with her at all. Her sewing machine was set up in the dining room. The constant whirr of the machine sang in my ears all day long and well into the night. She worshiped Chana and was attentive to her every need. I felt that my grandmother received far more attention from my mother than I did and was more important!

Edzia took great care over her appearance; she was a picture of chic elegance. No matter what she was doing, whether at home (working at the sewing machine), shopping, washing up or going out on errands, she looked fabulous, as if she were ready for the theatre!

To be honest, I don't remember much about my father. He was much older than Edzia. Although he had been very handsome when he first met my mother, the picture I have in my mind is of a balding man with a large, rotund tummy. In comparison, Edzia seemed young, slim, always well turned out and stylish, energetic and forever on the go. She never stopped. Her feet barely touched the ground.

Ilia, on the other hand, tended towards indolence. He was not a dominant character, like Edzia. He was more than happy to step back and leave all of the responsibilities to my mother. I do not remember him ever helping her, not even lifting a glass off the table to take to the kitchen. He lay on the couch, falling asleep. He spent hours reading the newspaper, not ever disturbing himself, whilst Edzia busily set the table, brought food from the kitchen, served everyone and then cleared the table after the meal before washing and drying the dishes and resuming her work at the sewing machine.

Edzia worked tirelessly at her sewing and with the salvaged knitwear machines: seven days a week until the early hours of the morning. She also did everything around the house, even bringing up the coal from the cellar. She did all of the DIY jobs. I remember her standing on chairs to change light bulbs and forever fixing things around the house. She did not have a moment to herself.

I don't remember my father, Ilia, ever going out to work or helping my mother with any household chores. Truth be told, he didn't lift a finger! He left it all to Edzia. And indeed, she took care of absolutely everything. She ran the house, provided for the children, took care of her ailing mother and put food on the table every day!

However, Ilia was in control of the money Edzia earned. He spent a considerable portion of it on Zionist organisations, Israeli charities and a Jewish choir, donating generously. He indulged his whims and sentimental leanings. At social functions, the absence of his wife was noted and commented on. So Edzia started to accompany him, from time to time, but she took little pleasure from these outings. They always had money problems.

I don't think Ilia took me to the park. And he never played with me. But I do remember that he would sing to me in Russian and Yiddish whilst stroking my hair.

Les enfants s'ennui le Dimanche
Le Dimanche les enfants s'ennui…

It makes me very sad to recall these words that he sang to me about children feeling bored on Sundays. Up to this day, every Sunday feels a little melancholic to me.

The knitwear machines make their final appearance

After the war, Edzia reclaimed the hidden knitwear machines. She may have sold some off and with those that she kept she began, once again, to start up a small business which she named after me.

These machines had been the lifeline of our family since the days of David Szklarz. Edzia worked tirelessly, churning out items of hosiery and knitted swimwear in the dining room of our home on Rue Marie Christine, day and night.

She worked until I left for Israel. And then she collapsed. She filed for a divorce and eventually re- married and moved to London.

Finally, the machines were put to rest.

Only in her dreams did Edzia hear the rhythmic motion and clack of the carriage as it spooled out endless reams of vibrantly coloured knitted wool.

Abandonment

My mother (Edwarda Szklarzowna, born on 15th January 1914, Warsaw, Poland) took her own life on 8th August 1989. She was 75 years old.

The Death Certificate reads:

Cause of death
Temazepam Overdose. She killed herself.

Behind those stark words there is a story too. It was not the war or the Nazis that had defeated Edzia. She had, in fact, remarried in later years and moved to London to live with her husband, Benny Goldbrom, enjoying many happy years with him.

However, during the latter years of her life, she suffered from osteoporosis. Her bones were so brittle that she easily fractured them. She was debilitated and in constant pain. Her sight was fading and she was becoming ever more dependent with each passing day.

I can only imagine that there came a point, when Edzia decided she had had enough. It was time to go. She had lived her life, taken care of and loved those closest to her. There was no more she could do. She was not prepared to carry on just for the sake of it.

Her suicide note to me read:
'Je regrette, mais je souffre trop'
'I am sorry, but I suffer too much'

Simple, sparing words that told the truth but gave me no comfort.

I found it on the little table next to her bed. Everything was neat, tidy and in order. Inside the envelope were her diamond ring and pendant (made from her mother's precious earrings that had been saved during the war). Next to this was an empty bottle of Temazepam. She had prepared everything in advance, without telling a soul. She acted alone, as she had always done. She had made up her mind.

She lay on her bed in her nightgown and she was gone.

I felt an indescribable feeling of abandonment and found myself tumbling down a bottomless, dark pit. The hidden child inside me cried out sharply (in a muffled sort of way) but there was no one to hear or break her fall. I could hardly catch my breath. I had been deserted. This was not a dream, like Alice falling down the rabbit *hole. This was not a tale from a children's story book and yet it was the story of a child. A child who feels hollow inside and who cannot stop falling. A child who feels powerless and who stifles her cries until they are deadened because there is no one to hear them. I am alone. I am frightened. I am abandoned once again. I have been left dangling.*

A grand-daughter remembers (Lena narrates)

I had spent many an hour with Edzia, my grandmother, listening to her stories about the past. We would talk in her house in London. She sat on the other side of the glass topped dining room table, tapping her cigarette holder against the purple glass ashtray. Yes, she still smoked, even then. The glass top was like a pool of smooth, glossy water between us. At the end of our chats, she would smile and say, '*Well, would you like a piece of cake now?*' There was always a homemade cake on offer.

Trails of cigarette smoke slowly and silently moved around the room like mist. The light would inevitably fade as the hours passed by, virtually unnoticed. It was getting dark outside. We carried on talking. When the lamp was switched on, the room took on a soft, yellow glow.

When I visited Edzia's home for the final time (after her death) I noticed there was some sewing thread on an armchair. The ashtray was empty and I rolled her cigarette holder across the glass table top. I tried to imagine Edzia's lovely, old face reflected on the surface of the glass. A shawl was draped over a chair. The silver candlesticks stood on the sideboard, dull-looking and in need of a polish. The plants on the windowsill were parched and needed watering. There was dust everywhere. It was very still and quiet.

When I left the house, it was getting dark. I turned around to give it one last look. I imagined hearing the whirr of a sewing machine and her lovely face watching me through the window, smiling, as the evening shadows closed in.

Edzia's memoirs were written in French, the language she had adopted as a young girl settling in Brussels with her family after their departure from Poland in 1930.

One day, as I turned over the loose pages of Edzia's diary (which described the events of her extraordinary life) a yellow star fell out, like a strange, autumnal leaf. The large, star- shaped, sulphur yellow patch of fabric (outlined in black with a Hebraic styled 'J' in the centre) was almost orange in colour. I was shocked to discover it and to imagine Edzia sewing the badge onto her beautiful coat with neat and precise stitches, hands trembling.

The Nazis ordered Jews to wear the yellow star to humiliate them and mark them out for segregation and discrimination. Later on, it facilitated identification for round ups and deportation to concentration or death camps. The yellow star was to be worn at all times and any Jew caught without one could be imprisoned or shot.

There would have been countless times when Edzia would have hidden the star behind a tightly clutched handbag or unstitched it from her outer clothing to get essential provisions or to travel. Certainly, this would have been the case when she visited Lydia in the Ardennes and Harry, who was also hidden in the countryside.

She had kept the yellow star all these years but had never shown it to me. It was caught in between the pages of her memoirs.

Edzia's yellow star

René Ferier: 9/09/1920- 16/03/2011

In Brussels, on 6th January 2000, René Ferier (aged 90) was awarded a medal and certificate of honour as a 'Righteous Among the Nations'. His name has a place on The Wall of Honour in the Garden of the Righteous at Yad Vashem in Jerusalem.

The medal of the Righteous bears the Jewish saying, 'Whosoever saves a single life, saves an entire universe.'

During the ceremony in Brussels, Lydia recounted her moving testimony.

René had been deeply touched by the honour bestowed upon him but always maintained that he was simply doing his duty and what his heart had dictated him to do, which was to stand up against horror and barbarity by saving a life. He always said that he simply did what any other decent human being would have done under the same circumstances.

Before this, René and Lydia had lost contact with one another. Approaching the age of 70, René had searched for Lydia and they were finally re-united, like a long-lost daughter and father in 1989. By this time Lydia was in her 50's living in London with her family. Much time had passed but it was also as if no time had passed at all. They would remain close until René's death on 16th March, 2011.

> *'I hope that this ceremony becomes engraved in the hearts of my children, grandchildren and great-grandchildren so that they may never forget how far a man can fall when intolerance, racism and hatred become his masters...'*

(An extract from René Ferier's speech given during the award ceremony, Brussels, 6th January 2000)

'J' ai deux pères. Celui qui m'a dit 'POUR QUE TU N'OUBLIES JAMAIS' et René qui m'a appris, par son

example, que la justice, la compassion et l'amour sont des valeurs qui vont bien au- delà des prejudges de race, de religion ou d' appartenance.'

'I had two fathers. One who said, 'NEVER FORGET' and René who taught me, by example, that justice, compassion and love are values which go far beyond racial, religious or ethnic prejudice.' (English translation of above)

(From Lydia's testimony, honouring René as one of 'Righteous Among the Nations' 2000)

Re-united after so many years: Lydia & René outside the family home in Bioul & the entrance to the chateau

By the end of the occupation, more than 40 percent of all Jews in Belgium were in hiding; many of them hidden by gentiles and in particular Catholic priests and nuns. Others were helped by organised resistance, such as the 'Comite de Defense des Juifs' (CDJ) which provided food and safe housing for them. Many of the Jews in hiding went on to join the armed resistance. Among the Belgian resistance fighters who were killed or executed, 244 were Jews.

The treatment of Jews was denounced by the senior Catholic priest in Belgium at the time, who described it as 'inhuman'.

According to the historian, Jean-Michel Veranneman, 'Belgium was one of the few countries occupied by Nazi Germany where a majority of the Jews (about 56 per cent) who were resident when occupation began, escaped deportation and annihilation mainly thanks to the help and devotion of many Belgians. Yad Vashem, the official Israeli institution studying the Holocaust, following strict criteria has identified over 1,500 Belgian 'Righteous among the Nations', mostly Belgian nationals or others who were active in Belgium (out of a total of 20,000 for the whole of Europe) and who were honoured thus for having saved one or more Jewish people.'

'Numerous Catholic priests and nuns hid and helped Jews out of Christian mercy... as did families of the Belgian nobility inspired by a sense of duty. Groups led by political, humanitarian or social ideals, clandestine Jewish groups and ordinary people from all walks of life listened to the voice of their conscience and goodness of their heart and acted accordingly.'[1]

---

[1] Belgium in the Second World War, Jean- Michel Veranneman, 2014, p.154).

Life goes in a new direction (Lydia continues her story)

It was not long after the war when Harry joined a Labor Zionist, secular Jewish youth movement called Hashomer Hatzair ('The Young Guard'). Of course, taking the lead from Harry, I joined soon after. And so started the beginnings of a new life. My father, Ilia, was not very keen on this movement as it was far too left wing for his liking. But we became increasingly involved with it over the years, until it virtually took over our lives.

I never really settled into school life after the war and found it difficult to adapt. Just like in Bioul, my school was situated opposite our house. However, I still managed to arrive late every morning!

I struggled to connect with the post-war patriotic sentiment that was high on the educational agenda at the time. Nothing I heard or learned seemed to resonate with my own personal experience. I felt different and was definitely open to something other than current mainstream thinking.

Hashomer Hatzair seemed to open up new possibilities and ideas, offer a new direction. There was light, optimism and hope which we grasped with both hands. We would become very idealistic, even militant, you might say. Hashomer Hatzair became our life, our belief system and our ideology. Our future would be shaped by it, providing us with the perfect antidote to our troubled past.

Meeting Guydon

I first met Guydon during one of the first Hashomer Hatzair meetings I went along to with Harry, always arriving on the back of his motorcycle. Guydon was a few years older than me. At the age of 16 or 17, he had already spent a year in Jerusalem, completing the 'Machon Youth Leadership Training Programme', where he learned about Jewish history and culture, Hebrew, traditional dances and songs. On returning to Brussels, Guydon became a leader in the youth movement and I happened to belong to one of the groups he was in charge of.

Needless to say, I was instantly drawn to him. He was warm, talented, inventive, charming and intelligent. He was completely immersed in and committed to the movement. The impact he had on our lives as a leader was undeniable. The fact that he was dreamily good looking, goes without saying! Handsome is too poor a word to describe him. He was Adonis! However, he was not vain in any shape or form. In fact, I doubt very much whether he paid any attention to his looks whatsoever or even realised how attractive he was!

Guydon would meet me outside my school at the end of the day and accompany me home. Then we would head off to meetings and events organised by the movement. I felt that I was the lucky one and the foundations of our relationship began to take shape.

He organised camping trips to the Ardennes where we would cook over open fires, play games, do exercise drills, sing and dance together. As a leader, he was there to support, educate, motivate, inspire and recruit youngsters to join the movement.

In reality, the movement was preparing us to make 'Aliyah' (Jewish emigration to Palestine) and for a life on a kibbutz in Israel, based on the philosophy and socialist ideology underpinning Hashomer Hatzair.

At the age of 18, we had to make a decision. Would it be university or the kibbutz? We had many debates about this in the form of a tribunal. The two opposing sides were put on trial to be examined and finally, to be judged.

The movement had taken over our lives and was a very powerful influence. It provided us with hope and a clear direction in which to move forward and build a post-holocaust future, from which we and our parents had survived but so many others had not.

The aim of the movement was to deter members from opting for a university education. They wanted to recruit as many people as possible to their socialist cause. They were selling the dream of the kibbutz and built-up images of an idyllic future.

However, looking back on this intense period, I can say that we were indoctrinated, even brain-washed. There is an element which I find quite disturbing about it all.

The reality of the kibbutz experience did not live up to my expectations. I feel that we were duped in some ways and sold a dream that did not exist.

Guydon and Harry went to Israel a few years ahead of me. Of course, I would follow them. My parents were not overjoyed by my decision. They would rather I had remained in Brussels to pursue my studies.

But I could only listen to my heart and there was absolutely no doubt in my mind that this was the direction I wanted to go in.

We had a dream and we intended to fulfil that dream. My parents couldn't argue with our desire to create a better world.

The orange that had been brought to us all the way from Chanan's kibbutz after the war had seemed to suggest a promise of some sort at the time. Now I knew what it had been: the promise of hope and new beginnings.

Post-war Belgium and Hashomer Hatzair

Edzia, Lydia, Ilia and Harry on the Belgian coast

Chanan (he brought the family an orange from Israel)
with Edzia, Lydia and Harry in Brussels

Lydia (holding the shield) with younger members
of the Youth Movement

Guydon (Youth Leader) and a little kitten – camping in the Ardennes

Lydia (18 years old) with Edzia and Ilia in Belgium, 1954

Lydia

Finally, the fulfilment of the dream- Guydon in Israel, early 1950's

Part 3 Guydon's Story- beginnings

Guydon Glinoer (my father) was born in Deurne, Antwerp, Belgium (26.12.1933) to immigrant parents, originally from a town in Bessarabia (now part of Moldova) called Yedinitz. Later on, the family moved to 24 Rue de la Poterie, Anderlecht, Belgium. His mother was Mariem Bluma Sapsis (born 22.12.1902) and his father, Moyses (Moishe) Glinoer (born 16.4.1901). The family were poor. No food was ever to be wasted. The children were taught to eat everything on their plates. There were quite a few mouths to feed with four boys! The eldest was Simon (born 18.4.1926), next was Abraham (born 24.5.1927) then Philippe (born 1.7.1930) and lastly Guydon who remained the youngest until Daniel, born in 1944, came along unexpectedly towards the end of the war. So, there would be five sons in total.

Theirs was not a religious home, although Mariem blessed the candles to start Shabbat every Friday evening. She wore a veil over her head as she uttered some words (perhaps prayers) in a hushed and reverential tone whilst performing mystical gestures around the flames. Moishe only ever attended the synagogue on Yom Kippur and Rosh Hashanah, but only because he felt obliged to do so as all of the other men in the community were present. It was an opportunity to chat and socialise. He was an atheist. He had no religious convictions whatsoever.

As a young man, Moishe had left Yedinitz to make his fortune in Sao Paulo, Brazil. He spent a few years there (joining others from his town) and finally returned with two chests filled with cloth, a valuable gift for his wedding! He returned as a hero and was known as 'The Man who Went to Brazil'! Dresses and suits could be made from these fine textiles. Moishe had done well! He was quite a catch and handsome to boot! He married Mariem, whom he had been betrothed to before he set out to make his fortune in Brazil.

The couple planned to return to Brazil after their marriage. On the way, they stopped off in Antwerp (1925), awaiting a ship to take them on the next part of their journey. However, Mariem found herself pregnant with her first child (Simon). Their plans changed and they remained in Belgium. 'Apatride' (Stateless) was stamped on their ID papers.

Moishe tried his hand at various trades. He did some tailoring and later on became a barber of sorts. Things were tight for the growing family, now there were three boys! So Moishe decided to try his luck in Brazil, once more. The plan was to make some money and then send for Mariem, Philippe, Abraham and Simon to join him there.

Mariem found herself pregnant yet again (with Guydon, her fourth child) and she refused to travel such a long distance in her condition. Moishe returned to Antwerp, not having carried out any of his plans or dreams in Brazil. He carried on cutting hair for a while until he acquired a market stall later on, after the family had already moved to the town of Anderlecht, selling items of hosiery and silk ties. As an adolescent, Guydon often helped out. Perhaps that's where his love of markets originated from and his compulsion to buy multiple packs of socks! It was hard manual work, as they would have to carry and transport heavy loads of merchandise each day and open up the stall during the early hours of the morning. The days were long and exhausting.

Guydon remembered, to his dismay, having his hair cut regularly by Moishe. But as a young boy, he preferred his hair to be left alone! Moishe would not hear of it and let the scissors do their worst! To the chagrin of all the boys, they ended up with very short fringes and severely clipped hair! Pudding bowl haircuts, the butt of many a family joke!

Moishe had many stories to tell of his escapades and adventures in Sao Paulo! He had picked up a little Portuguese whilst there and had many fond memories. There had been one striking photograph of him taken in Sao Paulo, a slim and elegant man clad in an immaculate white suit wearing a white Panama hat (unfortunately, I have been unable to locate this image). If only the family had joined him whilst he had been in Brazil. They would have been spared all the suffering and horrors of the war when Belgium was occupied by the Germans in 1940.

However, if Moishe and Mariem had remained in Yedinitz (then part of Romania), they would have fared far worse, as the following extract explains.

> *Approximately 315,000 Jews lived in the counties of Bessarabia, Bucovina and Dorohoi, according to the last official census of December 1930.*
>
> *The German army attack began on July 2, 1941, along the entire length of the Romanian border, from Bucovina to the Danube. Along the path of the fascist army, looting and slaughter among the Jews occurred on a massive scale. In Yedinitz, mass killings of Jews took place on 6th July and the corpses were buried on 7th July in three mass graves. Of the 5-6 thousand Jewish residents in Yedinitz, one thousand people were murdered during the first two weeks of the occupation. The Romanians established a concentration camp there, by enclosing the Yiddish part of the shtetl (small Jewish town or village in Eastern Europe) with barbed wire. On July 25th, a consignment of 25,000 Jews from northern Bessarabia was transported across the Dniester to Ukraine, and left to wait in an open field in horrifyingly overcrowded conditions.*
>
> *Altogether, it can be concluded that two months after the beginning of military actions by the Nazis, at the end of the first phase of their 'holy war', approximately 150,000 Jews were missing, killed or had perished as a result of bestial persecution, starvation, thirst, fatigue, untreated diseases and wounds, etc.*

> *On September 16th, after less than two months, a great number of Jews had died in the camps of Secureni, Edinti, Vertujeni and Marculesti.*
>
> *On November 15th, the Nazis declared that the first phase of the deportations had ended. The camps in Bessarabia as well as the ghetto in Kishinev had been emptied. After November 15th, 1941, not a single Jew was killed in Bessarabia: there were none left!*
>
> *('The Holocaust Revealed' 2003)*

Mariem and Moishe lived and worked mostly amongst the Jews within their own community. Mariem only spoke Yiddish and Moishe spoke enough Flemish and French to get by. The boys grew up in a non- religious, Jewish, Yiddish- speaking household. Guydon was very attached to these roots. He spent the first 6 years of his life in Antwerp. As time passed, the family moved from one apartment to another (more often than not basement flats which were cheaper to rent) in order to accommodate their growing family, until they finally settled in Anderlecht (a suburb of Brussels).

Mariem was a traditional Ashkenazi housewife. She prepared wholesome meals for her family from her homeland: chicken soup with kneidler and kreplach, baked carp, potatoes, chicken pot roasts, carrot tzimmes, sweet pastries filled with poppy seeds, chocolate, fruit or cinnamon, savoury pastries filled with meats, cheese or potato, pickled vegetables, jams and marmalades. For adult consumption only, she prepared glass jars filled with cherries soaked in alcohol which fermented into some sort of liqueur. The family were poor but they always ate well and food was plentiful. Theirs was a close-knit family. The boys lived in a home with a lively, warm atmosphere. Their parents were hard working and devoted to them.

Moishe was a stern and serious man with high moral standards. He brought up his sons in a strict fashion and expected them to be decent and responsible at all times, good and helpful, hard-working, trustworthy and honest. He tried to instil his own values within them. He was fastidious in all things, including his personal attire and the home, where everything needed to be orderly and ship-shape. He would not tolerate misdemeanours from his sons. They could expect severe punishments if they transgressed. The merest suspicion of bad behaviour would be reason enough for Moishe to take his belt to one of the boys! The good name and reputation of the family were very important to Moishe. There was a strong ethical code to uphold, which was woven into the fabric of the Jewish community within which the family lived.

Guydon had a sense of orderliness as well as chaos in later years, both forces moved within him. As a boy, he had been as bright as a button and was full of promise! There was something about him: charisma, charm, energy, mischief, boundless curiosity and intelligence. He may have been a little shy and unsure of himself sometimes, vulnerable even. His dark eyes could look at you with depth, intensity and a hint of melancholy. Something about him shone out brilliantly though, like the rays of the sun, touching everyone. As the youngest son, I imagine he was permitted a little more leniency than the others.

He was a well-behaved boy at home, doing what he was told. He spent many long days playing in the street with the other kids. Philippe wanted to be with the older group and tried to lose him, running off with his bigger pals!

After the war, they would climb over and rummage through mounds of rubble, searching for treasure. The boys returned home covered in grime, with rips in their shorts and pockets bulging with 'finds'.

Once, he and Philippe entered a shop to steal four large, very beautiful stamps illustrated with fine and detailed drawings of Spanish Armada Ships. Out of nowhere, a hand reached out and grabbed them by the scruff of the neck! They had been caught red handed and were hauled off to the office! No doubt, stern words were uttered to scare them. Guydon was in fear of going home, as he knew he would have to face his father's wrath. He expected to be beaten! Fortunately, nothing came of it. The shopkeeper did not report the incident to Moishe. The boys had had a lucky escape and would never attempt anything of the like again!

Guydon recollected spending a lot of time at the port of Antwerp as a young boy with his brother Philippe and a group of friends (during the first 6 years of his life before the family moved to Anderlecht). He watched the big ships come and go; the loading and unloading of cargo. To occupy themselves, the boys invented a special tool. They tied a piece of Mariem's sticky laundry soap onto the end of a pole and tried to pick up things that passers-by may have dropped accidentally through the open grilles in the streets. They spent hours fishing around with their improvised rods, prodding, scraping and poking, sometimes finding pennies, a ring or other objects of interest! To them, it was all treasure trove!

Sometimes, Guydon would ask Moishe, *'But where did we come from before Yedinitz?'*

His father didn't know exactly. He couldn't trace the family any further back. So Guydon's imagination fired up, like a hot air balloon rising higher and higher up into the sky as the burner dispenses heat. He started wondering and wandering inside his mind. Wanderlust was ignited! He imagined that perhaps they were descended from a long-lost and ancient tribe from Mesopotamia or even Africa!

Guydon only had vague recollections of Abraham and Simon. The eldest, Simon, was a bright, tall and good- looking boy. He was helpful, good- natured and considered a real asset to the family. Abraham, however, was viewed as a burden. He was always getting into trouble, committing petty thefts and generally behaving in ways that earned him great disapproval from his parents. He was seen as 'problematic' in some way. Further than this, Guydon was not able to elucidate.

The beginning of the war and the loss of Abraham and Simon

When war broke out, Guydon was 6 years old. All he remembered from that early period was that everyone seemed to be shouting around him. There was heightened excitement and tension in the air when the newspaper headlines announced the outbreak of war. But as a young boy, he didn't understand the significance of this. The family were now living in Anderlecht.

At the beginning of the war, the family travelled to the Belgian coast, where they thought they could escape the German invasion and find safety. Guydon remembered long convoys of people trying to leave Brussels, on foot and by car, possibly trying to get to the French border (just as Edzia had tried to do with her own family). He remembered being down a cellar and hearing the muffled sound of bombs going off. Another early recollection was the sight of a dead body- a soldier who looked huge, black and swollen to him (possibly charred from an incendiary bomb). Those were his only recollections about the beginning of the war, as a small boy.

Eventually, the family returned to Anderlecht, only to discover that Belgium had fallen into the hands of the German army. Passports and ID cards were stamped with a large 'Yuden' in wet black ink and soon Jews would be ordered to wear the yellow star so that they could be identified in the street. It was not long before the German authorities issued the order for all single Jewish males to present themselves for compulsory work (in effect, forced labour). Initially, the Germans were careful to present themselves in a more benign light so that the Jewish population would be more likely to acquiesce and less likely to resist. They assured Jewish communities that the menfolk who were being sent off to work would be permitted to send money home to their families.

Also, a rumour was circulating that if families went along with the German orders, parents would be spared the same fate. Most people went along with this, not realising at this stage, that people were being deported to concentration and extermination camps.

The two oldest brothers, Abraham and Simon, were sent away by order of the German authorities under the decree of forced labour (Service du Travail Obligatoire). They were held briefly in Mechelen Transit Camp, Belgium, before being deported to Auschwitz Birkenau extermination camp, Poland on 4th August 1942, where they were sent to the gas chamber and murdered on the day of their arrival. Simon would have been 16 and Abraham 15 years old.

At the time, Guydon's parents knew nothing of this. They had followed orders, like so many other families. They wished to avoid antagonising the Nazis, believing that they were keeping themselves safe in the only way they could and that their sons would eventually return home to them.

Why didn't Moishe and Mariem have the same instincts as Edzia about the imminent peril they were facing? It would seem that they had not possessed that kind of intuition and, catastrophically, made the decision to follow the order to send their sons away.

However, as information about the death camps started to filter through to the Jewish community and the Germans stepped up their activities (no longer hiding behind the guise of a tolerant occupying army), families searched for ways in which to save their children from the clutches of the Nazis and certain death. At some point, Moishe and Mariem must have thought the unthinkable: that they might never see their two eldest sons again and that they were possibly lost to them forever. On the other hand, perhaps this way of thinking was simply impossible. They could not allow such thoughts to enter their minds.

A turning point

Guydon described how, one evening, as a young boy, alone with his mother at their home in Anderlecht, there was a deafening pounding at the door and the sound of loud German voices. Two soldiers entered, demanding to see identification papers, whilst shouting at Mariem to get ready and pack immediately. The soldiers' bulky presence and loud voices in the small hallway must have frightened and shaken the young boy. These giant figures seemed to fill the space entirely, sucking out all of the oxygen and light. Guydon's mother begged and pleaded with the soldiers to spare her as the family had already sent away their two eldest sons. One of the soldiers threw the papers on the floor in a gesture of disgust and anger. Then they left. The sound of heavy, booted footsteps rang in Guydon's ears as he dragged a chair to the window and stood on tiptoe, trying to follow their movements up the external steps from the basement flat into the street above which was eerily empty, having been sealed off at both ends. He just about caught a glimpse of the soldiers' gleaming black boots when some residents from his block (carrying suitcases and bundles filled with clothes and possessions slung over their shoulders) came out onto the street followed by German soldiers pointing guns into their backs. They walked silently out of their ordinary and everyday lives into an abyss of the unknown (probably never to return home again); the soldiers' barks forcing them towards the open mouth of a grotesque and salivating ogre, waiting to devour and destroy. Suddenly, Guydon was pulled away from the window by his mother's strong grip, the chair toppling over. He heard the footsteps trail off. Mariem lit a candle with her trembling hands, whispering strange incantations through her tears.

Guydon described this incident as a kind of miracle. It was unheard of for a German soldier not to carry out orders to arrest Jewish citizens whilst conducting raids. No exceptions were ever made. He felt that he and his mother had escaped the Nazis 'by the skin of their teeth'.

After this incident, Moishe and Mariem wasted no time in sending their two youngest sons, Guydon and Phillipe, to a hiding place in the countryside whilst they too went into hiding for the remainder of the war, moving to the attic of the house they were living in. The Keysers, an elderly couple who also lived in the same block, helped them survive through the war.

With the support of a Jewish organisation and help from the Belgian population, Guydon and Philippe were first sent to a safe house in a village called Cul-des-Sarts, Province de Namur, on the border with France. They were placed with a group of other young Jewish children. Guydon had sketchy and vague memories about his time there. However, what is clear is that he was very unhappy. He remembered how the unappetising food turned his stomach. Soggy vegetables, very little meat and meagre portions left him hungry. He remembered the lumpy, turnip soup which seemed to stick in his throat and lie heavily in his stomach like a stranded whale. He remembered suffering from stomach cramps and heartburn.

He pined after his mother's soft matzah balls swimming in hot, golden lokshen soup and the little kreplach parcels filled with meat and mashed potatoes that melted in the mouth. He dreamed of the rich, sweet apricot jam he used to stir into his tea at home.

Perhaps Moishe and Mariem had tried to send the boys parcels of food, as so many parents did during that time, whilst their children were placed in hiding.

How long he and Philippe stayed there is unclear. Guydon remembered much more about the second hiding place in Jamoigne (Ardennes). Altogether, the boys would be separated from their parents for two years. The only communication they had with them was through letters addressed and posted to Mrs Kayser (who passed the letters on to Moishe and Mariem who were hiding in the attic). All this was organised to avoid detection by the Germans, who were hunting down Jews everywhere.

Guydon and Philippe spent the remainder of the war in a Catholic boarding school in Jamoigne, in the Walloon region of Belgium, close to the French border in the south of the country.[2] Whether this had been organised by the Jewish Defence Committee or the underground movement, I do not know. Before leaving home, the two brothers (my father must have been around 10 years old and Philippe a few years older) were told by their parents to be good boys but never to forget who they were and where they came from, in spite of having to hide their Jewish identity and take on new names. How much they really understood about their situation, I cannot say. Guydon had hazy memories of his time in Jamoigne. He remembered that he and his brother were given the surname: Kayser. They had taken the name of the couple who lived in their apartment block so that letters could be sent to their parents via them. Guydon was now known as Jules Kayser. This was not to be the last time he assumed an alias.

> 83 Jewish boys were hidden amongst the non-Jewish pupils in the Catholic boarding school, 'Reine Elisabeth', housed in the Chateau du Faing between 1943 and 1945. The school was run by the Principal, Emile Taquet, with his wife, Marie. In 1987, along with all of the staff (including teachers and counsellors), they were awarded the honorary title of 'Righteous Among the Nations' by the State of Israel in recognition of non-Jews who had risked their lives to save the lives of Jews during the Holocaust.

The school (run like a summer camp) was modelled on the scout movement and followed similar rules. My father remembered that different age groups were given names from characters in 'The Jungle Book': Mowgli, Baloo, Bagheera, Shere Kahn, Raksha, Kaa, Akela. This must have made an impression on his young and

---

[2] Guydon and Philippe's names are listed in the book 'La patrouille des enfants juifs- Jamoigne 1943- 45' Dominique Zachary (Editions Racine): both their Jewish and war names are listed at the back under Annexe 1 Liste des enfant de Jamoigne retrouves (69).

imaginative mind. He also remembered that he never forgot his parents' words and secretly clung onto his Jewish identity, as if his very life depended upon it. During daily church services, he refused to sing the hymns and prayers along with the other children. Instead, he made up his own prayers to his own god, under his breath. He put Jesus, Mary and the Holy Ghost to one side, whilst speaking to and preserving his own made- up god. He scratched out the communion wafer with his nails until his tongue bled. He was steadfast in his endeavour to preserve his identity and never forgot his parents parting words. He kept his mind strong and focused, never succumbing to this 'other' religion. His secret mission was to remain true to his roots and family.

He remembered learning to tie knots and participating in lots of organised outdoor activities. There were drills and marches, exercise routines, leaders and flag bearers. The school camp was run in a regimental way. The system was hierarchical and strict. Philippe was in a group with older children and, I think, Guydon resented this separation. However, he always knew that his brother was never far away and would look out for him.

At home, the family only spoke in Yiddish. When he arrived at Jamoigne, he spoke a smattering of French and Flemish. But Guydon was a bright boy and learned fast; soon he would be writing poems about beautiful sunsets in French. He was told that he had some talent as a writer, which made him glow with pride. Consequently, he would sit by one of the windows in the chateau for long periods at a time, staring dreamily or studying the changing seasons with great earnestness for one so young. After all, isn't that what a poet was meant to do? He sent his parents poems and wrote one for his teacher, all in French! The kindly couple, whom Philippe and Guydon were now named after (Kayser), brought the letters sent from the boys to their parents and read them out, as Moishe and Mariem's capacity to read and write in French was limited. The couple also scribed the replies from the parents and posted them off, minimising the risk of detection.

Words dropping from the sky, return home and a surprise

Guydon never once described to me how splendid and impressive Le Chateau du Faing in Jamoigne was. In fact, he never once mentioned there was a chateau there at all. When I came across it in photographs much later on, it was indeed like something out of a fairy tale with its turrets, gables and towers, set within its own forest and gardens. The children at the boarding school, 'Reine Elisabeth', would have had access to this outdoor space. But perhaps to this small boy, it would have all seemed intimidating, unfamiliar and confusing. Everything was on such a grand scale. The refectory was set up in the Armoury, the dormitories occupied the Grand Hall with its imposing, stone fireplace. He didn't know whether he would ever return to his family home or see his parents again. He looked up at the Coat of Arms and all he understood was that he would never relinquish or allow himself to forget who he really was and where he came from.

Towards the end of the war, Guydon described leaflets dropping out of the sky. The boys jumped up and down, trying to grab them as they floated down. Philippe read out the words to him: LIBERATION IS IMMINENT... as the allied planes disappeared into the clouds overhead.

When the war ended, Guydon remembered seeing American tanks driving through small villages in the Ardennes and lots of jubilant shouting.

Eventually, he and Philippe would return home to their parents, who had survived the war thanks to the brave and kind actions of the Kaysers. They had expected to find their two older brothers waiting for them too. But Simon and Abraham were nowhere to be found. Instead, a new baby brother, Daniel, was waiting for them, a beautiful little boy with piercing blue eyes and a head of bright blond hair!

From the ashes of the holocaust (the death of Simon and Abraham) emerged a new and precious life. To some degree, the unexpected birth of their 5th child must have softened the pain Moishe and Mariem had to endure. They remained with three treasured sons. The victor was not 'brutality and destruction' but love, after all.

There was a big age gap between the youngest child, Daniel, and his elder brothers, Guydon and Philippe, who were 10 and 14 years older than him.

In time, Philippe and Guydon would join the Zionist youth movement, Hashomer Hatzair, becoming ever more involved with it. They were growing up fast and developing lives of their own outside of the family home.

Philippe married young, soon to start a family of his own. Guydon was totally immersed in the youth movement which would eventually lead to his emigration to a kibbutz in Israel in 1954, at the age of 21.

Daniel remained at home with Mariem, her youngest boy. If he had been especially well behaved, she would treat him to a tall glass of sour milk mixed with a pink, sweet, grenadine syrup made from pomegranates which she purchased at the market where she did her daily shopping. He remembered her as a warm and affectionate woman. He only had happy memories from his childhood. By putting the past behind them, Mariem and Moishe were able to move forward, focusing their energy and love on their three remaining and dearly beloved sons.

There are some photos of seaside holidays Daniel took with his parents on the Belgian coast. For Moishe and Mariem, spending some days by the sea, breathing in the salty air, paddling in the water and sitting on deckchairs in the sand was always a delight! A simple pleasure which they never tired of, a million miles away from the bleak shtetl in Yedinitz which had been situated so far away from any glimpse of the sea.

Little Daniel, the miracle of the war, would become a doctor and eminent endocrinologist.

Whilst Guydon was living in Israel, the family in Brussels was preparing to visit him on his kibbutz in the Negev desert. Daniel had turned 17. However, at the last moment, Mariem declared that she did not feel well enough to travel and stayed behind.

Once in Israel, they received a telegram to say that Mariem had been admitted to hospital and was quite unwell. They cut their visit short. On the way home, they learned that she had already passed away in Saint-Pierre University Hospital, Brussels, in the year 1961, the same hospital Daniel would work in for most of his career as a doctor.

A letter to Philippe

A whole lifetime later, from his home in London, my father thought of the following words after his older brother, Philippe, died at the age of 86. Guydon could not attend the funeral in Brussels, being very unwell himself at that point. He barely had the strength to gather thoughts together, let alone write anything down. He who had once been such a talented little poet! I think he must have dictated these words (originally in French) to my mother who typed them up. I don't know if they were read out at Philippe's funeral.

> *Hey Philippe! Hello my big brother. What a journey you and I have been on! How many times did you take me by the hand, steering me through times of such difficulty and hardship.*
>
> *It all began at the Port of Antwerp: you with your chums and me scared to be left alone. Then we grew up a bit. And then came the filthy war; both of us hidden children in the countryside. Cul-des-Sarts, Jamoigne: me with the little ones and you with the big kids in these so-called 'summer camps'. Far away from our parents who were being threatened by the Germans. But we were not caught and escaped the worst!*

I was not alone because I knew that you were never far away and I was protected.

"Get lost, you idiots and cretins! My big brother's coming to get you!" We got through it, you and I. We lived through it together.

After surviving the war, there was Hashomer Hatzair. Once more, me with the little ones and you a leader in training.

And then we grew up a bit more: you with your lovely wife and I well on the way to becoming a pioneer (Halutzim) in the land of Israel…

Somehow, it would seem that we learned to exist a little apart from one another as the years went by. But in fact (and we always knew this) we remained close and united. I close to you and you just as close to me.

There are all sorts in the Glinoer family. You are the one with common sense, generosity, humour and, dare I say, humanity. You were special; your wisdom enriched all of us.

Goodbye, bon voyage…

(English translation from French, 2017)

To me, these simple and fragile words reveal what had stayed in Guydon's mind at the end of his own life, as he was to pass away only a few months after Philippe, at the age of 83. Guydon recalls the closeness between them, the bond that could never be broken, the older brother who took care of him and defended him during the most difficult times. Guydon never felt alone because Philippe was always there, never far. It is an expression of love and gratitude from the lips of a frail and dying man to his older brother, remembering the past they once shared.

I always thought Guydon should have been the one to write a book. He had all the makings of a writer: intuition, perception, talent, instinct, experience and insight. And what a life he had lived! When we had discussed this in the past, he always gave the same explanation: he could never get beyond the first few lines, sentences or phrases as he battled to get every word and nuance perfect. It was an impossible task!

In hospital, in a terribly weakened state at the end of his own life, Guydon had scribbled down some words (barely decipherable) in scratchy, spider-like strokes. My mother had encouraged him to write things down. He hardly had enough strength to hold the pen. The same fate would befall her too, in the end.

Guydon and Lydia had written so many letters to one another in their youth, after Guydon departed for Israel as a young pioneer (just a few years before my mother joined him). Their deepest thoughts, hopes and desires flew on the air from Brussels to the Negev and from the Negev to Brussels, passing each other like ships in the night. Their tender words written on thin translucent pages of writing paper like the gossamer wings of trembling moths flying through darkness towards a place of tremulous & diaphanous light.

Simon and Abraham Glinoer- lost sons, brothers and uncles

These are the bare and stark facts I know about my uncles, Simon and Abraham Glinoer, who were lost to our family in 1942 at the hands of the Nazis.

They were born in Antwerp, Belgium: Simon on 18th April 1926 and Abraham on 24th May 1927.

They were the eldest sons of my paternal grandparents, Moishe and Mariem, who would go on to have three more boys: Philippe, Guydon and finally Daniel. Tragically, Simon and Abraham would never know of Daniel's existence because they were both murdered by the Nazis after their deportation from the Mechelen Detention

Camp in Belgium to Auschwitz Birkenau Extermination Camp, Poland on 4th August 1942. Daniel was born two years later.

The chilling facts leading up to their murder at the hands of the Nazis are recorded in the archives of Yad Vashem under 'The Central Database of Shoah Victims' Names'. The information on Simon is listed under Item ID: 7846548 and on Abraham under Item ID: 7846547.

The details found here are from a Deportation List from the detention camp at Caserne Dossin in the Flemish city of Mechelen. It states their name, gender, place and date of birth, citizenship (Stateless), profession (Simon is 'without profession' and Abraham is a 'fur tailor'), the detention camp they were both held in, the date and destination of deportation (Auschwitz Birkenau Extermination Camp, Poland) details of transport (Transport 1), prisoner transport numbers (Simon- 270 & Abraham- 269). We know that they were both murdered immediately upon arrival at Auschwitz.

The floodgates opened. Is this it? But there is so little information. The single word 'murdered' was a slap in the face, a kick to the stomach, a sledgehammer bearing down.

So many questions and images raced through my mind. These records (holding such scant information) nevertheless deliver the news of their deaths with force and impact. The truth is brutal and unequivocal: they were murdered. The gaping holes, blanks and gaps belie a tsunami of savage violence, brutality and horror.

I never knew my paternal grandparents. I can only imagine the utter devastation when they realised that their sons would never return. I do not think they would have dared to ask themselves the question, but how did they perish? Perhaps, for a short time, they believed that their sons would come back to them. But as time passed and hope faded, Abraham and Simon were made to vanish into thin air so that life could continue and be possible.

I was told that after the war, it was absolutely forbidden to mention Simon and Abraham's names in the family home. It was as if any recollection of their existence had to be stifled in order for life to go on. They would be made to disappear. Perhaps it was Moishe and Mariem's only way of being able to live with the terrible tragedy and a deeply buried feeling that they had (unwittingly) played a part in sending their two sons to their deaths.

After the Germans conquered Belgium, the military administration gradually started following the same anti- Jewish policy as in Nazi Germany and the 'Mechelin Transit Camp' was to play an important role in this. Between October 1940 (a few months after the German invasion of Belgium in May) and September 1942, many anti- Jewish regulations were imposed upon the population, gradually excluding Jews from all aspects of social- economic life. The first step was compulsory registration and identity cards were marked with 'Jood- Juif'. Out of an estimated 60-70,000 Jews living in Belgium at the time, 55,670 were registered in this way. Most were foreign refugees (from all sorts of backgrounds, both religious and secular) having escaped persecution and anti- Semitism in other parts of Europe. Thanks to these lists, the Germans knew about Jewish activities and the whereabouts of Jews in Belgium. The implementation of 'Judenpolitik' (the Nazi policy against the Jews of Europe) was underway. On 27th May 1942, a new regulation required all Jews to wear the yellow star (explicitly seen as a component of the 'Final Solution'). By the end of 1941, the 'Association of Jews in Belgium' (AJB) or 'Judenrat' (Jewish Council) was established. Using the AJB as an intermediary of the German orders to the Jewish community served Nazi tactics well, whereby Jews were made to participate in the persecution policy. Careful not to offend public opinion and the Belgian administrative authorities at first, the occupiers acted with a degree of measured restraint. They were relying upon cooperation in order for their plans to run smoothly. In 1942, however, Nazi activities began to escalate as the implementation of the 'Final

Solution' was set in motion. Jews were summoned, rounded up and eventually hunted down to be taken to the Dossin Barracks in Mechelen. At first (in order to avoid alarm and suspicion amongst the Jewish population) the Nazis ordered the AJB to distribute call-up notices or work orders (totalling almost 12,000) to the Jewish population. They even provided a list of items to pack before departure in order to reinforce the impression that people were actually being sent away to work. They were instructed to bring provisions for 14 days: non-perishable rations such as oat flakes and canned food, work boots and overalls. Thousands of Jews answered the call-up, many fearing possible reprisals if they disobeyed.

The first Jews arrived at the Dossin Barracks by truck on 27th July, 1942 and the first convoy left Mechelen just eight days later on 4th August, 1942. Jews got on the train voluntarily, believing that they would be employed elsewhere. Simon and Abraham were on the first transport out of the detention camp, having no idea that they were being sent to a death camp.

Jews arriving at the detention camp in Mechelen were assembled in the large courtyard as they disembarked from the transport trucks. The process of dehumanisation (typical of the Nazi persecution system and a clear move towards extermination) began immediately. Each detainee was forced to hand over every single identity paper or card in their possession. These were destroyed. They were also forced to hand in all personal possessions, including family photographs and letters. Their details were recorded on the infamous 'Transport List'. Every single detainee underwent a physical search which often degenerated into gratuitous violence towards male prisoners; groping, indecent assaults, humiliation (such as being stripped naked in public) and sexual abuse against women. Then their luggage would be thoroughly checked. Finally, they were issued with carboard signs with their serial number for the convoy, which they were to wear around their necks at all times.

The Jews were divided into different groups. Abraham and Simon were in the group to be deported immediately ('Transportjuden').

After a three- hour long registration procedure, the detainees were given a blanket, a plate and a spoon. They were forced to live in degrading, over- crowded and unsanitary conditions, strongly resembling life in a concentration camp with regular roll calls. Lice, fleas and outbreaks of disease were common. The food served to prisoners was poor and meagre (bread and soup), resulting in hunger, weakness and poor health. Families sent food parcels if they could but prisoners did not always receive them. Detainees were often humiliated, insulted, abused and beaten. The camp was known for its extreme brutality.

Transport 1 had 544 men, 28 boys, 403 women and 23 girls, totalling 998 people. Abraham and Simon were amongst them. Their names had been replaced with numbers as they boarded the freight wagon which would be referred to as 'The Death Train' by the prisoners of subsequent transports. Only 9 people survived from Transport 1. People on later transports wrote letters and final words on scraps of paper to their loved ones (being only too aware of their fate) which they slid out between the wooden slats of the wagon. Their final hope would be for those words to somehow reach home.

25,490 Jews and 353 Roma were deported from Dossin Barracks on 28 train transports to Auschwitz- Birkenau between 4th August 1942 to 31st July 1944. Few survived the ordeal.

I presume Simon and Abraham were gassed together at Auschwitz Birkenau, immediately after they disembarked from the transportation train which arrived from Mechelen on 4th August 1942. Simon was just 16 years old and his younger brother, Abraham, only 15 years of age. To the Nazis, Simon and Abraham were invisible, simply two more sets of numbers on a check list to be marked off and sent on their way to the gas chamber. Not one guard or soldier cared to look into their eyes to discover that they were human, just two young boys (not dissimilar at all to their own younger brothers back home perhaps).

Simon and Abraham had not been held long at the Mechelen detention camp in Belgium. Detainees were processed quickly and efficiently so that as many people as possible could be deported to the death camps. As the train slowly passed through the hellish gates of Auschwitz Birkenau (after a long and terrible journey in a cattle car) their fate was already sealed. They were set on the conveyor belt of death from the very start of their journey. There had only ever been one final destination.

How long did the journey from Mechelen to Auschwitz Birkenau take? Many long and tortuous hours, no doubt. The horrific and inhuman conditions inside the cattle truck are unimaginable. No food, water or air. Suffocation and darkness. People on their feet and tightly packed together for the entire journey. There was no room to move. People grew weaker, increasingly unwell and sick. They must have fallen on top of one another with exhaustion. The hellish conditions inside these transport trucks have been well documented by survivors. When the train finally screeched to a slow halt after passing through the main entrance of the death camp, was it day or night? Was there hysteria, panic, desperation, commotion and screaming as the boys alighted the train at gun point, surveyed by the watchtower guards and greeted by a pack of barking, snarling, snapping dogs straining at their leashes. Or was the unfolding scene strangely quiet, unravelling in slow motion? Fear had taken hold and a sense of what was to come barely allowed for the slightest hush or intake of breath. Pulses raced erratically or had slowed down to a faint, almost undetectable rhythm. Did Simon hold onto Abraham tightly, for fear of losing him? Did he remember his parents parting words: always look after your brother. What passed through his mind?

If they had arrived in the middle of the night, I imagine floodlights blinding and disorientating them. If they had arrived in the day, was it a warm afternoon with a hint of summer in the air? Abraham thought a butterfly wing brushed against one of his cheeks when, in fact, it was grey ash. The stench of death was overpowering and clung to them. No birdsong in the woods beyond the barbed wire. The forest was silent and colourless when it should have been full of wild summer flowers and bees. The skies burned red. How smart, clean and pristine the soldier's uniforms looked with their gleaming black leather boots.

The German guards barked their orders: get off the train, leave your luggage behind.

I imagine that Simon took care of his younger and more fragile brother. Simon was smart and good natured, responsible and dependable, the pride of the family. Abraham, on the other hand, was troubled, simple and vulnerable.

I imagine him holding onto Abraham firmly and talking to him in Yiddish, their mother tongue, in a steady and reassuring tone. He may have told Abraham stories or spoken about the family. He may have told Abraham not to worry and that all would be well. Perhaps Simon uttered a prayer under his breath, although he had not been brought up in a religious household. He would not be parted from his brother, though.

Maybe I am altogether wrong. Perhaps Simon was frozen with fear. His beautiful, intelligent, warm brown eyes glazed and hardened with terror and uncertainty. Perhaps his head was spinning. Perhaps his hands trembled uncontrollably and the beating of his heart galloped wildly as if it might burst from his chest. Perhaps a throbbing, stabbing pain pulsated between his temples. The scene before him was both blurred and as sharp as steel, glinting under the sharp beams of sunlight or cruel slashes of moonlight.

> The selections in Auschwitz took place immediately. Families were divided after leaving the train cars and everyone was lined up in two columns: men and older boys in one column, women and children of both sexes in the other. SS doctors and other camp functionaries then judged who was qualified for labour and who was to be killed immediately. These decisions were made by sight. Sometimes they elicited a brief declaration as to a person's age and occupation. And upon this, they decided who would live or die. Age was one of the principal criteria for selection. As a rule, all children under 16 years of age and the elderly were sent to be murdered in the gas chambers. Of the approximately 1.1 million Jews deported to Auschwitz, about 900 thousand people were killed in the gas chambers. Women of child bearing age and children were especially targeted. This was the essence of genocide: preventing a human group from having a future.
>
> After the selection process was completed and the people were marched off, either to their deaths or forced labour, prisoners in striped uniforms clambered onto the cattle trucks and threw down the suitcases that had been left behind, many of them breaking open on impact with the ground, their contents spilling out.
>
> Piles of shoes, suitcases, clothes, jewellery, silver items and all manner of personal belongings were immediately sorted through by other prisoners in large warehouses: the stolen possessions of an innocent people whose only crime was to be born a Jew. Millions of ordinary people were brutally abused, enslaved and murdered for this reason only.

Moishe and Mariem had parted from their two beloved sons, believing that the only way to keep the family safe would be to follow the Nazi decree: single males were instructed to leave their families to work elsewhere. What else could Moishe and Mariem have done? What choice did they have? No one defied Nazi orders (apart from Edzia!); they had no idea about what was really happening at that point in time. They believed the whole family would have a better chance of surviving this way. The true meaning of 'compulsory work' meant slave labour in a concentration camp or being sent to one's death. This realisation would soon come to light, as the Nazis did not keep up the pretence for long.

The Nazis were liars and brutes with lopsided grins and twisted grimaces painted on their faces like demented, malevolent clowns. In reality, of course, they were ordinary looking people. Their murderous intentions were hidden underneath piles of mundane paperwork and amongst the millions of names on their endless lists. Nothing could be more sinister than the seemingly ordinary bureaucracy of the Nazis, so thorough, meticulous and deadly. Simon and Abraham were 'lambs to the slaughter', like so many millions. Two innocent and dearly cherished boys, brothers and sons from a loving family, at the epicentre of the most barbaric and heinous episode ever recorded in history. They were at the mercy of the murderously racist Nazi machine; trapped within the frothing jaws of degenerate men with outwardly respectable appearances in pristine uniforms who sought to exterminate an entire race of people by committing mass murder on a mechanised, industrialised and bureaucratic scale never seen before. The Nazis had quotas to fill. It was simply a question of numbers, accounts and efficiency at the end of the day.

Mechelen Detention Camp, Belgium

New arrivals of Jews, Roma and Sinti at SS-Sammellager Mechelen (Dossin Barracks) would be processed through the Aufnahme (Registration Department). Some of the administrative employees of the camp had been recruited amongst the young Jewish girls who had arrived when it first opened. Work at the Aufnahme was divided into two sections: the administration of the camp and the confiscation of Jewish property. Without a doubt, Abraham and Simon had arrived at the detention centre with suitcases packed by Moishe and Mariem containing the items on the list provided by the AJB by order of the occupying Germans. The two ID photographs show the boys looking smart: donning pressed shirts and ties, warm jackets and having neat haircuts. Moishe and Mariem wanted them to make a good impression to give them the best chance. Abraham is facing away from the camera (cross-eyed) but Simon, the eldest, looks straight into the lens with his intelligent eyes, soft mouth and swept back, shiny, thick hair. He is a loving & gentle boy, you can see it in his face.

The employees at the detention camp, mainly inmates themselves, worked day and night to process all of the newly arrived prisoners as quickly as possible. They also drafted the deportation lists, distributed cardboard identification tags, physically searched newly arrived detainees and completed confiscation forms. During the first phase, all information on the newly arrived prisoners was added to a system of index cards. In the second phase, the deportation lists were drafted. At least 4 copies were made: the original was sent to the SiPo (German Security Police - major perpetrators of the Holocaust)) in Brussels, a second one was kept at the Aufnahme, a third one was handed over to the staff of the deportation train and a fourth one was sent to Berlin.

There exists a carbon copy (most likely that belonging to the Aufnahme) of the original transportation list from SS-Sammellager Mechelen with the names of Abrahma and Simon printed on it. There are ten names on the sheet. Abraham and Simon are the last two, at the bottom. At the top of the page is written: 'TRANSPORTLISTE - 1 27.' Abraham's name is registered after number 269 and Simon's after number 270. The page is printed out in purple ink on yellowish paper. It states the boys' date of birth and that they were both born in Antwerp, that they were Stateless, that Abraham was a fur tailor and that Simon had no profession.

The Aufnahme continued to operate until liberation of the camp on 4th September 1944. As liberation drew near, the lists of the detainees were hidden and saved from destruction by a Jewish member of the administrative staff at the camp.

A letter to Simon and Abraham,

Know how much you have always been loved, remembered and cherished, never forgotten. Serial or ID numbers are not all that remain of you. You are Simon and Abraham, beloved sons of Moishe and Mariem, brothers to Daniel, Philippe and Guydon. You have faces we can see and a story that we ponder over. Yes, your end was violent; your young lives senselessly cut short at the hands of thugs, criminals and murderers, lost to your parents and younger brothers who were expecting to see you again. But you never returned home.

It is true that it was forbidden to mention your names ever again after the war. Moishe and Mariem had to banish you from their thoughts so that life would be possible for them.

You were snatched away (your young lives snuffed out like candles), stolen and destroyed by acts of unimaginable depravity, cruelty and inhumanity. But severance did not take place. Connections could never be broken. Impossible for you to be forgotten. Your place within the beating heart of the family could not be dislodged because it had never been removed in the first place. That would have simply been impossible. You have always existed. Monstrous actions do not triumph over acts of love, even if no one dared to speak of that love or barely whisper it within the labyrinthine entanglements of a dream.

A fragile, breakable, terrifying, beautiful, secret, hidden and excruciatingly painful love that we must dare to recall so that you may both be remembered and liberated from a place of darkness and shadow, from the forbidden, unspeakable and unutterable.

I am breathing life into you so that I can remember you. I see you in those last two photographs, taken in 1942 just before you were killed, as if frozen in time. Two precious sons who were robbed of the chance to live and become old men. It is only through remembering and naming that we thwart anonymity and the ultimate objective of the Nazis: annihilation that would leave no trace.

The Glinoer Family

Pre- war photograph of the young Glinoer family (dressed in their finest) with Moishe standing at the back & Mariem sitting down surrounded by her precious boys. Guydon is the youngest child (holding onto Mariem), Simon is the tallest with Philippe in front of him, Abraham has his hand over Mariem's arm

Philippe and Guydon (best friends)

Daniel (youngest son born during the war) & Guydon, Belgium, 1950

Proud parents (Mariem and Moishe) visiting Guydon in Israel, mid to late 1950's

Moishe and Mariem enjoying a paddle in the sea, post-war Belgium

Guydon, Philippe and Daniel together in Brussels

Simon (16 years old)   Abraham (15 years old)

ID photos held by Mechelen Transit Camp before the boys' deportation to Auschwitz Birkenau on 4th Augsut 1942
(Yad Vashem, Digital Collections)

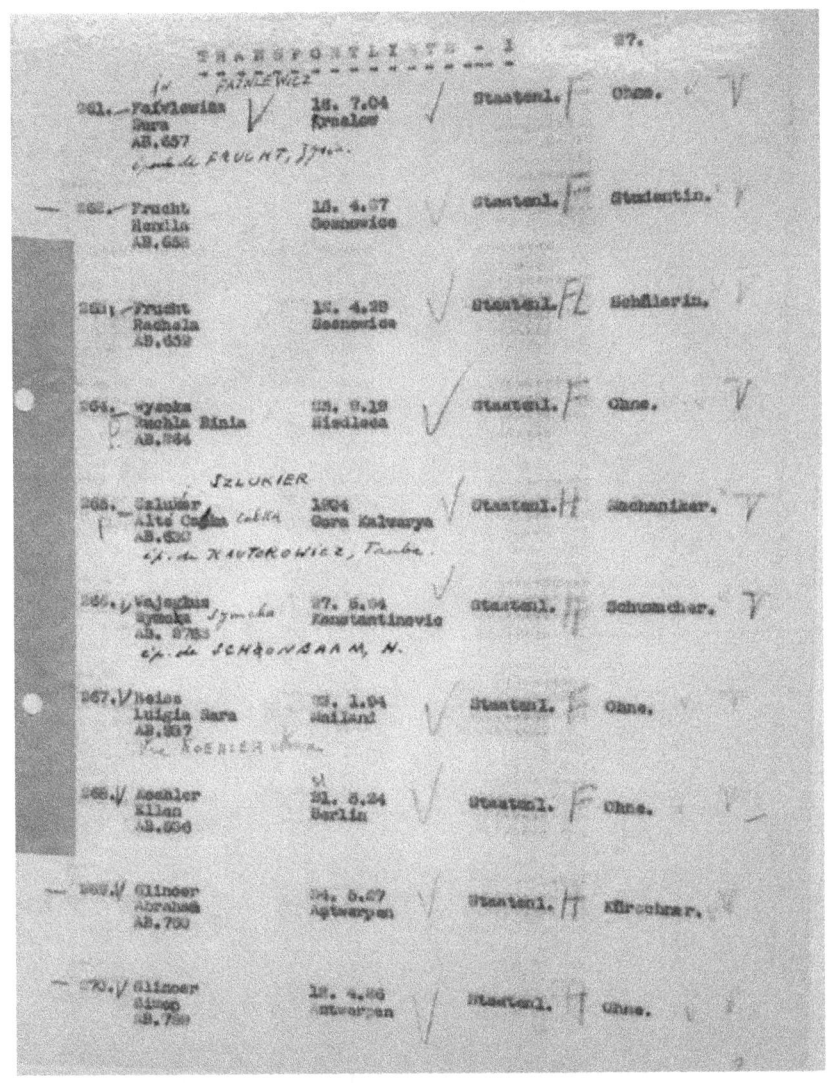

Transport List 1 from Mechelen transit camp- Abraham & Simon are the last two on the list after numbers 269 and 270 (Yad Vashem, Digital Collections)

Part 4 Glimpses into my early childhood, the story of the kibbutz and the last weeks of my mother's life

I used to make kibbutz cake with my mother, Lydia, whilst I was growing up in a North London suburb in the 1970's. She had previously lived on a kibbutz in Israel with Guydon, my father, for about 10 years from the early 1950's onwards. My older sister, Eldar, had been born there. The kibbutz cake recipe (see appendix 2) was created for the children of the kibbutz, during those early years when strict rationing was in place. Real chocolate was unavailable so one had to be inventive with whatever ingredients one could get hold of. I can tell you that this is a very delicious cake, although a little tricky to assemble! So, although I myself had never lived in their kibbutz as a child, the making and eating of 'Kibbutz Cake' made me feel less excluded from this unique experience, which I regretted that I had missed out on and not been a part of.

My early childhood in North London, 1970's

The only knowledge I had of my parents' life in the kibbutz was through stories and photographs. I remember poring over the 'kibbutz albums' as a child with feelings of longing and fascination. I had played no part in this other existence which did not resemble, in any shape or form, the life we were living then in another country entirely. We were renting a three bedroomed flat above a parade of shops in a prosperous and, predominantly, Jewish area of north London. However, we were not part of the affluent community whom my parents had very little in common with. A wide stairwell needed to be ascended from the main street before reaching our front door. Then on entering the flat, you would need to climb up another set of steep steps to reach the first floor where our accommodation was laid out. Our flat had a long, narrow corridor running through it, wallpapered with an orange embossed 70's style pattern. At the front, overlooking the shops and main road, was my tiny box room and a square shaped living room. The windows rattled every time lorries went by and when left opened, the noise from the busy road invaded the rooms, muffling our voices. At the other end, overlooking the garages at the back, was the kitchen. Two further bedrooms and a pink bathroom suite completed the layout of the flat which you accessed off the long, dark corridor between the kitchen and lounge. You couldn't get from one room to another without passing by someone in the narrow and windowless hallway. Eldar (my older sister by six years) and I did our utmost to ignore one another, whilst at the same time, being acutely aware of the other's presence. Indeed, we would have much preferred to be able to pass through one another like spectres, gliding along the hallway and disappearing into our bedrooms. There was a feeling of claustrophobia and tension within those walls. Something weighty, painful and melancholic hung in the air. My sister and I secretly eyed one another with suspicion and mistrust. I wondered what had happened to the happy kibbutz child I had seen in the photographs? She was nowhere to be found. Instead, a sour and wounded figure crossed paths with me along the gloomy corridor, trying to make me disappear out of sight and mind.

The kitchen was the brightest room, enjoying rays of direct sunlight. Once, Guydon attempted to grow an avocado plant from the fruit's large seed. He pierced the sides with 4 cocktail sticks so that the seed's belly just touched the surface of the water as it balanced on the rim of the drinking glass. He placed it on the windowsill, hoping it would catch enough sunlight and warmth to grow roots, which it eventually did. They trailed underneath the seed like thin, white worms or a sea anemone. This was a world away from when Guydon had farmed large swathes of land in the Judean desert as a young man fulfilling the dream of making

Aliyah (emigration to Israel). Now he was reduced to a single windowsill, it seemed to me.

As children, we would sometimes play in the courtyard at the back of the block of flats, where the garages and locked up shop yards were (as there was no garden space). We had both been bitten quite seriously by a neighbour's Alsatian (ex- police dog). I had been bitten on my right cheek, the dog's teeth narrowly missing my eye. He was owned by a family who lived in the same block as us, on the other side of the stairwell. The dog would come out with the children and we would all play together. He just went for anything that moved, particularly children running after balls. I remember being taken to the hospital to have stitches, screaming with terror. The incident was reported to the police. When they came to interview me, they said that I had the right to ask for the dog to be put down. But I decided against this. It seemed unfair. To my mind, it wasn't the dog's fault. His owner was the father of the children we used to play with: an unfriendly, hostile and racist man who filled me with fear. He was the one to blame, I thought. He should never have allowed the dog to be taken out to play freely with other people's children (being only too aware of how dangerous he was).

When this man ran into Guydon (my father) on the stairwell, he would make aggressive remarks such as, *'Why don't you bloody well go back to where you came from!'* He did not hide his contempt for this foreign looking and sounding family who had recently moved into the block. Guydon always stood up to him and there were times when an encounter with this neighbour came close to fisticuffs.

Further reflections on childhood

Home was my sanctuary from the outside world when I was growing up as a child. There was safety and familiarity there. Shelves were crammed with many books written in languages

I could not read, French and Hebrew. There were novels of classic literature, poetry anthologies, books on collecting antiques, dictionaries, reference books and many art books. There were also the photograph albums from my parents' time in Israel, which I frequently got down from the shelf and scanned with enthusiasm and interest. Good food was central to home life. Lydia was a fabulous cook!

However, the food served up at my primary school was alien to me and I regarded it with deep suspicion. Lunch often consisted of thin slices of fatty, gristly beef drowning in a grainy, sticky gravy with a scoop of mashed potatoes and soggy cabbage on the side. The smell turned my stomach.

Desserts were equally appalling to my mind and taste buds. A thick, gloopy, bright yellow custard seemed to accompany every single pudding, whether it be a compote of stringy, sharp-tasting rhubarb, jam roly-poly or ginger cake. The only dessert I found remotely tolerable was chocolate sponge with an accompanying chocolate custard.

Mostly, I would stare down at the food presented to me in distress. Unable to contemplate putting anything into my mouth, tears would soon well up which made swallowing impossible. The lumpy custards and water-logged vegetables drowning in gravy seemed like terrifying, steamy swamps swimming before my eyes whilst terrible and poisonous gasses wafted up to me. I felt the eyes of the other children upon me like sharp, hot pinpricks. Adults loomed over me: *'You can't go out to play until you finish what's on your plate!'* What a herculean task lay before me! Eventually, they dismissed me, probably out of pity.

I couldn't wait to finish school and get home at the end of the day. Here I found all things familiar and comforting: real food, Guydon's warmth and gentle humour, shelves crammed full of interesting books, a fascinating and eclectic collection of objects from my parents' travels which told their story.

Guydon was brilliant at choosing the best watermelons. He tapped them all over (not unlike a doctor performing a medical examination), listening out for that perfect hollow sound. And indeed, when sliced open, they were fragrant and sweet.

The heatwave of 1976 gave my parents no trouble at all. They adapted to the weeks of unusually high temperature naturally. They felt at home once again. It brought them back to a time in the past when they had been full of hope, youth and energy, living a different life entirely and inhabiting a different world.

Another brief glimpse into a childhood home

What I also remember about our home above the shops (apart from the continuously rumbling traffic at the front, which only quietened down on Sundays and later on in the evenings) was a sense of uniqueness. It was unlike anyone else's home in the neighbourhood. It was filled with treasures from other times and places which gave me a glimpse into past lives. Fascinating objects were scattered around the flat from my parents' travels in Morocco, Paris and Israel: a Bedouin copper coffee set, pieces of Berber jewellery, hand beaten brass jars, a red Moroccan leather writing set edged with intricate gold patterns, a large amethyst crystal, cloisonné oriental candlesticks (one depicting a black Chinese dragon, the other exotic flowers and butterflies), French lampstands fashioned from beautifully smooth glass (sinuous and liquid-like) and two large red and black Moroccan leather pouffes. Fresh flowers were arranged in old, hand-painted vases. Guydon would bring more treasures from the London antique markets he frequented and loved so much: Portobello, Bermondsey, Camden Passage, Covent Garden. These were regular haunts of his.

My early impressions of another life in the kibbutz

The black and white photographs of the kibbutz, taken by my father, Guydon, all those years ago, held a certain mystique for me. Everyone and everything seemed to be bathed in a golden light. Most of the images captured outdoor scenes with my mother and Eldar (a baby and young infant) as the central figures. There were tantalising glimpses of kibbutz life and the surrounding landscape: the little white concrete house my parents shared, my father's cactus garden, little birds drinking from saucepans filled with water that my father left out on the small veranda, the dry and parched earth, vast space, tinder dry grasses, the glimmering swimming pool with its Monet style Japanese bridge in the background, farmland and tractors, undulating fields of golden wheat, immense skies, the Red Setter they adopted, endless swathes of sand, flowering wadis, moon-like rock formations, the other-worldliness of the Sinai and beautiful sun kissed children.

Kibbutz Gvulot is located in southern Israel, in the north- western Negev desert, not so far away from the Egyptian border. Armed guards patrolled the electric fences each night as the danger of being attacked by hostile Arab factions was real and present. Irrigation equipment (vital to their subsistence) needed to be protected. Lydia had described seeing carpets of wild black irises in the distance. These rare flowers display a unique mix of colours characterised by a dark, almost black purple with a mesmerising lilac hue. Spring blooms grew wildly amongst the rocky crags and crevices after rainfall.

Here was a world, a million miles away from our dreary suburban existence, from the cold and constant drizzle and overcast leaden skies which seemed to oppress me. A world without the slabs of grey, uniform, concrete pavements. The kibbutz albums painted a picture of a different era, before my time. A place bursting with light and enchantment which I could only imagine. A world full of delightful promise, which I achingly and secretly yearned for. A world which seemed to offer freedom and all things beautiful. A world which did not contain that weighty, melancholic something that I found skulking in the shadowy corners of our flat. A world of endless space and dream- like landscapes. A world populated by happy families, living together in perfect harmony.

Was the kibbutz real, I asked myself? Had it actually existed? Or was it a fabulous dream? A figment of the imagination? I continued to wonder as I slowly turned the pages.

Lydia's arrival in the middle of the night

A few weeks after her departure from Brussels in the 1950's, Lydia finally arrived at the port of Haifa, after a long voyage by sea which had begun at the port of Marseille. Harry (her cousin from Belgium) was waiting for her in the kibbutz truck. It was already late and there was a long journey ahead of them. The two large wicker trunks Lydia had travelled with from Brussels were loaded onto the back of the truck amongst spilling sacks of grain and they set off on their way. When they finally reached the Negev in the middle of the night, Harry placed a gun between them on the seat. They had entered enemy territory where invisible and hostile Arab factions were present. They continued driving in darkness in the middle of the desert. Suddenly, Harry put the hand break on and announced that they had arrived. Lydia thought, arrived where exactly? There is nothing here! They seemed to be in the middle of nowhere! She had not expected any of this and was woefully unprepared! Harry hopped out and opened the door on Lydia's side and she stepped onto sand! She was taken by surprise. Had she landed on the moon?

Lydia was following on from my father, Guydon, who had already been in Israel for two years. She was about 20 years old, young, beautiful, in love and full of idealism. She had been dreaming of this moment for a long time! Finally, she had arrived, a young woman about to embark on a new life! Following her heart, dreams and beliefs, she felt close to the possibility of escaping the long shadows the war had cast upon her.

Desert nights are black. She could discern very little through the inky darkness. She stepped out of the truck and inhaled the cool night air. She never forgot that first introduction to Kibbutz Gvulot. The sand! The constant chirrup of cicadas. The thick, impenetrable night shrouding everything in darkness, like a magician's black cloak. What might be revealed a few hours later, when darkness melted away? And where on earth was Guydon? She had travelled all this way to be with him, after all!

Travelling the Silk Road

Later on, I thought of Guydon as a traveller on the Silk Road, no matter where he was or what situation he was in. Guydon was always voyaging (inside his mind and imagination) from one place to another or, driving his taxi in London from the 1970's onwards, discovering treasures on the way to bring home to share with us. He never stopped this 'mental journeying', even at the end of his life when he became so ill. In some ways, he roamed even more then, as his life had diminished and become so restricted. Perhaps the internal travelling began when he was a boy, during the war, to escape and dream. And then a dream turned into reality when he finally went to Israel as a young man. He was a wanderer. He did not put down roots. He was known to be able to lay his head down anywhere and fall asleep. He adapted. Guydon once said that his capacity to adapt to different situations was both a quality and his downfall.

A kibbutz in the middle of a desert

Kibbutz Gvulot was initially named Mitzpe Gvulot. It was the second modern Jewish settlement in the Negev and the first of three 'look-outs'. It was founded in 1943 by immigrants from Romania and Turkey who were members of the 'Kibbutz Eretz Israel Gimel' group of Hashomer Hatzair. Its original purpose was to guard the land owned by the Jewish National Fund, research the soil and climate of the region and assess its suitability for agricultural use. In 1946, it was recognised as a kibbutz.

The Negev is a rocky, stony desert, receiving very little rain. Mountains are interrupted by wadis (dry riverbeds that bloom for a brief time after the rains) and deep, lunar-like craters. Kibbutz Gvulot is surrounded by seemingly endless expanses of sand and rocky valleys. The surrounding landscape possesses a sparse, desolate beauty which bewitches anyone who dares to live there and is never forgotten. Bordering the Sinai Peninsula, one could unwittingly step over onto Egyptian land, as all deserts flow into one another, merging like seas.

Vast swathes of blue sky meet sweeping carpets of sand and undulating rock formations on the horizon. As the nights close in, streaks of purple, orange, pink and magenta stain the sky, bathing the hills and mountain ridges in warm hues, spreading like ink. Black nights pricked with sharp little stars create a dome above the kibbutz, like a child's snow globe. Desert cicadas disturb the thick silence with their distinctive vibrating sounds. Nights are a heady, dense, black treacle. When the temperature plummets, the desert becomes a cold, dark and freezing planet. The distant cry of a jackal pierces through a dream, splintering the night.

Life in the kibbutz very much centred around the children. The community was devoted to them. They were, indeed, the precious seedlings from which the future sprouted and verdant forests would grow.

One member from Switzerland donated his entire inheritance to the kibbutz and they built a 'club room' with an espresso machine, in memory of his parents. This provided the community with another communal area, purely for relaxation and socialising. There was a corner for periodicals with a choice of newspapers and journals. Comfortable chairs and tables were arranged around the room. Members could chat, play board or card games, listen to discussions and lectures. Movie nights were organised for the enjoyment of the members who could watch foreign films on a projector.

The kibbutz had various farm animals, including chickens, cows, goats and a horse.

Pathways crisscrossed the kibbutz, interconnecting all the different areas, including the adults' quarters, the children's houses, the communal dining room, the swimming pool and the 'club room'. Plants, shrubs, flowers, grass and trees were planted to create areas of garden, greenery and shade all over the kibbutz.

Faluja: two perspectives

Guydon had not been there to welcome Lydia because he had been working several miles away in Faluja, where the kibbutz had leased some land owned by the Jewish National Fund to cultivate crops. Kibbutz Gvulot was not in an area that could be farmed easily, due to very arid, desert conditions and limited irrigation.

Guydon might be absent for a fortnight at a time with a team of other workers, labouring 12 to 14 hours a day under the blistering Middle Eastern sun. They always carried guns to protect themselves from possible Arab attacks. After some time, he was put in charge of the entire operation. He organised the network of irrigation pipes that crisscrossed the fields, helped to prepare the soil, took care of the dozen or so tractors and repaired them when needed (his mechanics diploma came in handy here), sowed and reaped, delivered food to the workers out in the fields, loaded heavy sacks of grain and generally drove around the vast area in the kibbutz jeep. He was attentive and helpful towards the young women who came along to prepare the meals and kept them company during the day. The network of irrigation pipes had to be moved manually (day and night) as there was no automated system in those days. The work was physically demanding and he absolutely thrived on it. He loved the feeling of being close to the earth. He enjoyed the whole process that was involved in growing crops of wheat: the ploughing, planting, reaping and harvesting. It was extremely satisfying and fulfilling to produce from the land. Never had he felt so alive; it would seem that this kind of life suited him well. In fact, they were some of the happiest days he remembered. Being in charge also meant that he enjoyed a certain amount of freedom which allowed him to make his own decisions, be master of his own movements and time. Nothing suited him better than this. They were successful in their farming efforts. Agriculture was pivotal to the subsistence of the kibbutz and contributed to the wider Israeli economy. The work Guydon did was essential and held in high esteem by all members of the kibbutz community and wider society. In fact, kibbutzniks were regarded as an elite group during this moment in time.

Lydia, on the other hand, saw things in a different light. She had once accompanied a team to Faluja. They brought a different girl along each time to prepare food and cook. She had found the conditions 'nightmarish'! The barracks they ate and slept in was infested with rats and there was rarely any hot water to be had from the old, rusty contraption they used. Conditions were pitiful, primitive and filthy and the work menial. She did not look back on this experience with any sense of romance or nostalgia. The girls were confined to the kitchen area for the most part, preparing food for the workers in the fields and then a big evening meal when they returned. She was alone for most of the day with only the rats for company. In the evening, the men returned dead tired from working long and punishing hours out in the fields. They showered with tepid water, ate and crashed out. Lydia slept in the middle of their quarters with the other beds forming a circle around her to protect her from the rats!

The Dead Sea Scrolls

'The Dead Sea Scrolls' were first discovered by Bedouin shepherds in 1946-7. The scrolls were housed in earthenware jars in a cave near to what is now referred to as the Qumran site. Since then, many thousands of fragments have been discovered in the Dead Sea area.

The Dead Sea, or Sea of Salt, is the earth's lowest elevation on land and the deepest hypersaline lake in the world. As one of the world's saltiest bodies of water, salinity makes for a very harsh environment in which plants and animals cannot flourish.

This area has attracted visitors from the Mediterranean Basin for thousands of years. It was one of the world's first health resorts.

It is located in the Jordan Rift Valley and is surrounded by mountains which do sustain life: ibex, hares, hyraxes, jackals, foxes and even leopards have been spotted. Hundreds of bird species inhabit the zone.

It has a hot desert climate and if ever there was a lunar-like landscape, you will find it here. It has a desolate and dramatic beauty all of its own.

Guydon always had an interest in ancient artefacts and archaeology. During his first years in Israel, he had volunteered to join an archaeological expedition near the Qumran site. He spent days ankle deep in bat and bird excrement shovelling it out of caves. On this particular expedition, nothing was found. However, some of the photographs he took capture the other-worldly beauty of this place.

There were many excursions through the Negev desert on foot. And on one of these, Guydon did discover something: fragments of ancient pottery buried in the sand which he wrapped in cloth. Those pieces of pottery eventually ended up in London, where they were finally glued together. A beautiful and ancient looking jar (possibly from the Mesopotamian era) was shaped out of the different shards.

The first years of Guydon's life in Israel were likely the best of his life. Here was a beautiful country to discover, steeped in history. He visited fascinating archaeological sites, ancient cities, fortresses and settlements: Yafo, Haifa, the Sea of Galilee, Jerusalem, Caesarea, Masada, Ein Gedi, Nazareth, Akko, Avdat, Beit She'an, Qumran, Capernaum and the Dead Sea.

He was simply passing through, as we all do in this short life of ours. The footsteps he made in the Negev desert have long since been erased by hot, dry winds. But there may yet be more shards of ancient pottery to discover there. Who knows what a slight change in direction of wind might unearth beneath the sand? The timeless beauty of the desert remains a constant and shifting background to so many changing stories.

The kibbutz treasurer

At some point, Guydon was appointed the kibbutz treasurer. This involved spending time away from the kibbutz and dealing with various banks in Tel Aviv whilst staying in the kibbutz flat. He juggled with the finances in order to keep them solvent and avoid bankruptcy! He arranged bank loans. He was successful at this. He enjoyed the independence and freedom the position afforded him. It made a change from his work in the fields and the regimentation of kibbutz life in general. Once business was taken care of, he was free to stroll around the city, enjoy some coffee and cheesecake, peruse antiquarian bookshops and go out to the cinema in the evening. There was time to relax, roam, dream and enjoy some simple city pleasures.

Ill health: the end is close

I feared going into the belly of the beast, as that is how I thought of the hospital at the time. We were at the start of the Covid- 19 pandemic in London. It was April 2020. The media was reporting on the daily death toll with increasingly stark and sobering numbers. I imagined the hospital as some kind of monstrous and dreadful Leviathan that would swallow me up. Courage was not one of my strengths and I have always had an over-active imagination.

I was very familiar with the ward Lydia (my mother) was on: The Walnut Ward. She had spent a fortnight there when she had first been admitted to hospital, a few weeks earlier. That was when we received the news of the incurable lung cancer. However, it was obvious that she had been grappling with ill health for months before that, battling with increasing difficulties over some time. However (as determined and stubborn as ever) she soldiered on. She had struggled with severe shortness of breath. The hacking cough was unyielding, in spite of four weeks of antibiotic treatment for a suspected bronchitis. She felt exhausted by these unrelenting coughing fits, which plagued her day and night, and could not be shaken off. The situation was worsening and becoming more difficult. Things at home had an air of neglect about them.

I received a call on Wednesday morning from the ward. It was 15th April 2020. A nurse's voice at the other end of the phone beckoned me to come to the hospital as soon as I could. *Do you live near to the hospital? Can someone drop you off? Best not to drive. Gather yourself together. I don't say this to everyone, but your mum is really special and I love your mum. I really love her. Pull yourself together and come.* I asked, in a very quiet voice, whether she thought mum was close to the end. *Yes, I think so...*replied the nurse. I had been waiting for this moment, not really knowing what to expect. I made my way there.

In fact, Lydia died two days later, on Friday 17th April 2020. The team taking care of her had not expected her to go on for that long. They described her as a fighter. They found it quite astonishing and were deeply moved by it. I wondered if she had hung on, in her semi-conscious state, for another chance to hear her daughters' voices one more time before slipping out of this world forever. Her heart remained strong for a little while longer, despite the cancer engulfing her.

She had been in hospital for a few days. I hadn't seen her since that fateful Saturday morning, when I discovered her sitting under the dining room table at home, half naked and in a bizarre world of her own. I called an ambulance. The last image I had was of her being lifted into the ambulance in her wheelchair with a surgical mask on her face. She looked like a very cross child, even with the mask partly covering her face. She stared straight at me with angry eyes, burning with reproach. Then the doors closed and they took her away. I was unable to accompany her due to Covid rules.

I had felt relief and a momentary surge of elation. The paramedics had thrown me a lifeline, a rope entwined with golden thread like Rapunzel's flaxen plait: thick, strong and unbreakable. I felt I had been saved. I 'prayed' that the hospital would now take charge and not send her back home, as I felt I couldn't cope with her illness anymore. We seemed to have crossed a line, an impasse had been reached. I felt as if she had been reeled in by an umbilical cord. My hope was that others would now take care of her needs during the last stages of her illness and that she would no longer be my responsibility. The disease was spreading like spilt ink across a white page. I was letting her go.

A beautiful voice

When I look at the kibbutz photographs now, I am in wonder at how lovely and beautiful Lydia was. Her hair is rich, soft, thick and dark. Her skin supple and smooth. Her features finely delineated. Her eyes a melting, pale brown. Her smile delicate, easy and warm. The timbre of her voice had been smooth and mellifluous, bell-like and crystalline. The world was unfurling before her like a ribbon of satin. She was so young.

Fear of the unknown

Into the bowels of the beast I go. There are security checks at the entrance to the hospital because of the Covid lockdown. I go in. The wide corridors are eerily empty, apart from a few doctors, porters and other medical staff. I know my way to The Walnut Ward. I have been there so many times that I'm sure I could make my way blind- folded. Something pushes me on, in spite of my fear. I reach the Respiratory Ward and go in. I fork off to the right and enter The Walnut Ward. As soon as my foot steps into that area, the nurse looks up from her notes and approaches me to confirm that I am Lydia's daughter. I say yes and start crying. She has been expecting me. She puts a hand on my shoulder and helps me with the flimsy plastic apron, tying it round the back. She tries to give me confidence and reassurance. She makes me feel safe.

She tells me that death is just part of life, it is natural. She talks to me as if I am a child, with kindness and understanding. She enters the small room with me, where Lydia lies on her hospital bed, her eyes shut. She tells me to speak to her: *She can hear you, she is responsive, I've been talking to her all morning, just speak louder*

When I walk into Lydia's little hospital room, all my fears evaporate and are forgotten. They drop at my feet like a broken string of pearls. The space feels containing and safe. Prompted by the nurse, I let Lydia know I am there. Then the nurse leaves us and I try to speak to Lydia, through choking tears and my face mask. All I can repeat, over and over again, are words of sorrow and remorse.

Her eyes flicker open for a brief moment as soon as I say my name. I am shocked by their colour: a cloudy, milky grey. The warm brown has seeped away. She seems to be searching for something: like the beam of a lighthouse scouring the lashing seas in a storm, trying to penetrate through dense fog and darkness. For an instant, she seems to escape from ever encroaching death. But so quickly is the mantle of death thrown back over her and she sinks beneath its weight once again. Her eyes do not manage to settle on me. There is no eye contact. She has the look of a blind person, searching (very momentarily) but not seeing or finding. Then her eyes close. It looks to me as if little, pale shells have been laid upon her eyelids.

The sheets and billowy pillows are spotlessly white. I am reminded of a scene, three years earlier. My father is terminally ill in bed at home, like a little sparrow with fragile bones one imagines could snap so easily, enveloped in the cloud-like featheriness of a white eiderdown.

Lydia is wearing a hospital gown. She is so clean. Her soft, silvery hair has been brushed and swept back, away from her face, revealing her still beautiful and fine features. The nurse comes and goes quietly. She busies herself with this and that, re-arranging the pillows and adjusting the position of the bed to make Lydia more comfortable. She is so calm, collected, focused and efficient in the way she goes about her work, attending to Lydia so much better than I ever did during the last stages of her illness at home. The room is quite bare. There are no machines anymore. This is the end. The very last part. It is very quiet. There's the bed, a little tray on wheels, a chair, the sink, a window and the pleated blue NHS hospital curtains drawn back. I notice a packet of incontinence pads on the chair. The walls are painted a light, lemony yellow. A gentle and warm breeze enters through the slightly opened window. It is a sunny, spring morning and a warm light filters into the room. I move the pads onto the empty tray and sit down to watch her.

The nurse comes in and tells me how she often brushes Lydia's hair because it is so beautiful. *Your mum has beautiful hair, I can't stop brushing it.* The nurse leaves and I watch Lydia. She sleeps. Her body twitches, particularly her arms, hands, legs and feet. She seems restless and agitated. And then, suddenly, a horrible groan escapes from deep inside her. A spasm seems to shoot through her body, as if there were some kind of writhing, electric eel inside her. Her body tenses, convulses and arches in pain. She seems to be wrestling with her illness and with death itself (a dark figure who was half- hidden in the shadows, waiting to snatch her away). Her eyes flicker open, very briefly, overcast with that grey, milky cloudiness. They close. The pain has passed. Her chest bubbles and crackles with every laboured breath. Her mouth is open, gaping and dark. I imagine it gradually engulfing her, swallowing her up whole into the muffled darkness of death. I am reminded of the cellar she feared so much as a little girl in Brussels. What monsters were in wait for her inside the yawning, terrifying, cavernous basement?

So here we are, Lydia and I. It is quiet and peaceful in the little yellow room. I imagine we are safe inside a walnut shell (just the two of us) within the infernal entrails of the giant beast.

Fleas and luggage

When Lydia stepped onto the cool, grainy sand all those years ago in Israel, she was taken by surprise. The night, pierced with glinting silver dots, stretched above her like black velvet. She inhaled the chilly air deeply, drinking it in like cold, black coffee.

Her first night spent in Kibbutz Gvulot would never be forgotten. Harry showed her to her quarters: a very primitive- looking wooden shack. Her heart sank and her dreams seemed to evaporate in an instant! Harry beamed with happiness as he explained that he had managed to get her a room all to herself. Most people shared! But this did not console her. He showed her where the toilets were, so far away! He brought her some food from the kitchen and warned her about the ditches, discarded farming equipment, barbed wire and possible attacks by the Fedayeen (Palestinian militants)! Then he kissed her goodnight. She wanted to go back home to Brussels immediately! She had not expected this! It was a shock. In the gloom of the darkened room, she tentatively sat down on the thin mattress. The rusty bed frame creaked. She tried to relax enough to lie down and shut her eyes. She pulled the scratchy blanket over herself. She tossed and turned, unable to sleep, feeling the springs of the mattress digging into her sides. She gave up! Fumbling about in the dark, she opened one of the wicker trunks she had travelled with and rummaged around inside, pulling out sheets, towels and clothes until she reached the chocolate which had been packed by Edzia. What a life saver this chocolate turned out to be! Lydia ate her way through two or three bars of delicious, half- melted Belgian chocolate to comfort herself through the night. She sat on the edge of the bed in a state of tension and apprehension. She dared not visit the loo! As she munched through the melted chocolate, the silence of the night was disturbed by muffled scratching sounds. She later learned that rats lived between the partition walls and under the floorboards of these flimsy-looking huts.

Early next morning, not having slept a wink, she was horrified to find her whole body covered in bites from top to toe. Mosquitoes and a whole host of unmentionable insects had feasted upon her during the night, parachuting down from every nook and cranny. She had been attacked by a pack of blood thirsty fleas, no doubt, living inside the mattress or blanket. She was appalled! Never had she imagined such things when dreaming of joining Guydon in Israel! He had written nothing about these conditions in his letters to her. And when would he finally show up? She asked herself what on earth she was doing in that godforsaken place. She wanted to return home.

She kept these thoughts to herself, though. Not even with Guydon did she share her initial feelings of horror, disillusionment and disappointment. She got on with her new life, like everyone else around her.

Lydia had expected and been prepared to work hard in the kibbutz. But she had been totally unprepared for these invisible enemies who tortured her over many nights and made her life an absolute misery. It was like a living hell!

Not once, during the war years, had she been bitten by a single bug!

At some point the rooms were fumigated, which seemed to do the job! Eventually they would be torn down and replaced with brick built, concrete dwellings.

First morning in Kibbutz Gvulot

After waking up covered in insect bites, Lydia stepped out of the wooden hut. It was very early in the morning. The light was tremulous, diaphanous and delicate. She just caught a glimpse of fading white, pink and lilac streaks. Soon the onset of soaring heat and the shock of metallic sun splitting through. No one had stirred yet. The kibbutz was cloaked in stillness and silence. She stepped onto the grainy sand with bare feet. She could have been at the beach! It was a relief to escape from the room of horrors. The cool sand felt good under the soles of her feet. The skies were immense here, rapidly changing in tone and hue, from pale and delicate purple to pink and then blue, as if an artist were throwing fistfuls of powdered paint at the sky. She breathed in the cool air which carried a hint of lemongrass on it. There were just a few rudimentary looking buildings scattered around the place and discarded bits of farming equipment. And then she caught sight of it! She couldn't be sure. It was uncannily fast and strange looking, a thing unknown to her. But then she was sure, after all. She imagined all sorts of unfamiliar creatures inhabited this desert land. A lizard (big, powerful and breathtakingly swift) ran across the path in the distance, before her incredulous eyes. It kicked up a fine spray of dust behind its running legs, sharp claws and muscular tail. Then it simply seemed to vanish into thin air, melting into the sand and stones.

Fateful words go unheard

At the end of Lydia's first stay in hospital (just a few short weeks before she passed away), I was sitting on her hospital bed with the young female registrar when we were given the news about the lung cancer. She pulled the curtain around the bed and the three of us sat close together, like we were camping out in a big, blue tent. The words were formed and delivered to us clearly. However, Lydia couldn't process the information. The lung cancer had spread and was incurable. There was no treatment. There was nothing that could be done at this final stage. A long shadow had been cast over our lives, much like the shadow lining her lungs. A death sentence had been proclaimed yet fell upon deaf ears. The path ahead was unknown and the end date a blank, much like our eyes: dull, empty pools. When the doctor left, we talked inconsequentially about this and that. I helped her pack before we left the hospital for home.

It had taken the medical team two weeks to detect her cancer. Two weeks of tests and biopsies, discussions and analysis. Cancer can be hard to find. It likes to skulk and hide in dark, shady recesses so that it can spread stealthily. I thought of the 'hidden child' whom Lydia had been carrying inside her since the war. The child full of secret fears and anxieties, anger and frustration.

Lydia had armour, seemingly forged from a fusion of the strongest of metals: titanium, chromium and iron. I suspect that she had begun to build this 'super-armour' as a hidden child during the war. It was invisible and, therefore, magical. No one could see it or touch it. It was indestructible! In her child's eyes it glinted like steel and was as hard and impenetrable as the snake's black obsidian, glassy eyes (a creature whom she would meet with, head on, at a different time in her life.) This armour repelled emotional pain and fear. She believed that it was necessary for her survival.

The greeting party

Lydia had arrived in kibbutz Gvulot with two large wicker trunks, organised and packed by her mother, Edzia, in Brussels. There were neatly folded blouses and skirts, cashmere twin sets (totally unsuitable for life on a kibbutz!), underwear, sheets, pillowcases, towels, soap, bottles of eau de cologne, toothpaste, coffee, sugar, tins of condensed milk and Belgian chocolate! Indeed, everything she thought her daughter might need in the middle of a desert, which was difficult to imagine from Brussels!

On the first morning, Lydia was welcomed by members of the kibbutz committee and the contents of the trunks were immediately claimed by the common treasury to be shared out amongst the kibbutz community. That was the regulation. She was handed a shirt (several sizes too small for her) and a pair of shoes (several sizes too large for her). And so began kibbutz life.

She didn't mind at all that the entire contents of her luggage were requisitioned and distributed. She had, after all, made the decision to be part of this communal and egalitarian way of life and she was prepared for this. What she found most difficult at the beginning, however, was a feeling of loneliness and isolation.

No doubt, she missed her parents and friends in Brussels. She would have liked to feel more supported by Guydon. His absence was noted and felt deeply. He spent long periods of time in Faluja, where the kibbutz grew most of its crops. She knew no one in the kibbutz apart from Guydon and Harry, who took her under his wing and looked out for her. She was very young and lacked confidence.

Guydon and Lydia had written many letters to each other before she joined him in Israel. Lydia was under the impression that they were, indeed, promised to one another. They were not betrothed, yet she believed that they were meant for one another. She had expected Guydon to be waiting for her, anticipating her arrival with longing. In reality, he had not been there to meet her on her first night. And he did not show up until days or weeks later. She felt forsaken and hurt, disillusioned and lonely. She was filled with a sense of painful disappointment; her expectations had not been met. However, she quickly put such thoughts out of her mind and got on with her new life.

Only many years later, did Lydia find the courage to ask herself whether her arrival at kibbutz Gvulot to join Guydon had made any difference to his life. He had been perfectly contented without her, it seemed. She, on the other hand, was full of romantic hopes and dreams. She had pined for him during their long separation, whilst he, it seemed, had adapted effortlessly to this new life in Israel without her. And if she hadn't come, what might have been?

Lydia was permitted to keep the two wicker trunks, which eventually ended up on the veranda of the small kibbutz dwelling she later shared with my father after their marriage.

First home together and a moment of pure magic

My mother and father's living quarters were modest and basic but at least there were no more rats, fleas or bugs to contend with!

The old wooden shacks had been burned down and new concrete dwellings were constructed to take their place. They didn't complain. This was progress, even luxury compared to what had been before! They shared one room with a door opening out onto a little veranda and garden. A small settee opened out into a bed. Neatly folded blankets and freshly laundered sheets were stored away. Bookshelves lined with French classics and a few personal possessions were fixed to the walls. A wooden crate was used as a small table upon which they had a radio, reading lamp, note paper, stamps, envelopes, a small gas stove to boil water for tea or coffee and an old tin filled with biscuits and small cakes. A Picasso print hung on the wall.

Guydon tended his little garden every day, where he grew red amaryllis flowers and cactus plants. One night, under the ever-watchful gaze of the moon, Guydon was able to capture something fleeting, secretive and wonderful. He had a way of getting hold of the ephemeral and magical. His camera flashed and went click. The moon blinked. A waxy- white, star-shaped cactus flower revealed itself for a brief moment under the silvery beams of the moon, captured on film for posterity. Guydon's little cactus garden, which only flourished once a year, was his pride and joy! Only one single flower bloomed during the night. And you had to be ready to seize the moment! By morning, it had vanished! It appeared very suddenly like an apparition, a phantom or rare underwater creature.

Gradually, orange-magenta streaks would break through the dark night like lava and leak into the new day, staining the cracked and flaking cream- coloured walls of the kibbutz houses. The cactus flower had closed up long ago. The kibbutz was stirring and readying itself for another working day. Only in the late afternoons and evenings would the little kibbutz houses be used for reading, writing letters or journals, secret books or poems. Occupants might play card games or chess, listen to music on the radio, draw and paint or play with their children. Small ghekhos flitted across the mesh covered windows and doors with lightning speed, their shadows crisscrossing in the quiet early evening hours of dusk and fading light, darting lightly and playfully across the minds of those who watched them.

A black snake in the children's house

Lydia's first job in the kibbutz was to water the gardens. After this, she was assigned a job planting seeds for the tomato crops. She found the work hard and physically demanding. She was issued with the regulation blue overalls and heavy, hobnailed leather boots which gave her painful blisters.

Lydia eventually ended up working in one of the children's houses where she assisted the 'metapelet' (full time child carer or nanny). One evening, as she was about to fill the bathtub with water, she saw a black snake poking its head out of the plughole. It flicked its tongue and stared at her with dark, shiny eyes, like two black cabochon gems. She quickly ushered the children out of the bathroom. Someone was called to sort out the problem. By this time, the snake had disappeared. Any visible holes were filled in with cement. Everything was checked carefully. It was safe for the children to return and have their bath. But later on, as Lydia was putting away clean clothes in the airing cupboard, there it was again, comfortably coiled upon a pile of towels, the very same black liquorice snake, with its glossy eyes and flicking tongue. The children were moved to another house for the night. She told me this story on many occasions.

Last few weeks at home

Lydia had spent two long weeks in hospital at the end of which we received the news of the terminal cancer. She had fought a titanic struggle whilst there, though, and was determined to get out. I suspect Lydia had not been altogether honest when giving her answers to the occupational therapist who was then able to tick off the required boxes to action a discharge. However, I saw how changed and weakened Lydia was and how difficult the road ahead would be. I was fearful. There were a lot of unknowns. I questioned the hospital about her discharge. With no additional support in place at home, I wasn't sure how we would cope. My anxieties fell on deaf ears, however.

Before leaving the ward, Lydia made sure she said goodbye to each patient, stopping by their bedside to have a little farewell chat and wish them the best of luck. So typical of her to reach out in this way with warmth, kindness and concern for others. She was so happy and relieved to be going home at last and after such a tremendous struggle.

As we waited for our ride home in the outpatient's lounge, I noticed how frail and unwell she looked, so much worse than any of the other elderly people there. My fears were not unfounded but I could not have imagined what lay ahead and that, in just a few short weeks, she would no longer be with us.

Lydia would spend three weeks at home before being admitted to hospital for the second and last time. Her deterioration came fast. She refused to sleep in her bed. She spent every hour of the day and night sitting upright in the armchair. She could do very little for herself. Getting to the lavatory became an almost impossible task. She had lost her smile and seemed far away. Her appetite dwindled with each passing day. She had no desire for food. I could barely tempt her with a cup of instant soup. Perhaps a glass of fresh orange juice or a small pot of yoghurt. She might eat a small slice of toast with French cheese, but it was hard for her to swallow the dry bread. She refused the fortified drinks that had been prescribed for her. She would only accept cups of freshly brewed coffee. She wouldn't hear of carers coming in to help a little. Her legs were swollen, thick and strangely shiny. She could hardly move. Her body was becoming more emaciated with each passing day. Her clothes were slipping off her shoulders, revealing protruding bones and sallow skin. She looked more and more as my father had done at the end of his life. I thought that death was approaching ever closer, hunched over her: a grotesque gargoyle, breathing its stinking breath on her bare shoulder.

There came a point of dread for me. When I came in the mornings (to open the curtains, switch evening lights off and prepare for the day ahead) I would find her doubled over, her hair hanging in front of her face like a curtain. More often than not, she wouldn't hear me come in. Eventually, she would lift her head up very slowly. Her skin was grey. She was rigid. It was as if she were turning into stone, petrifying overnight. Her eyes were dull, almost lifeless. A thin line of dried blood, the colour of rust, traced the contours of her mouth. There were tissues spotted with blood scattered around her on the carpet. Increasingly, other objects were dropped on the floor during the night which I would find on the carpet or under her chair in the morning: reading glasses, torn Co-codamol sachets, her mobile phone, the remote control. Everything had slipped out of her hands like soap. Her pyjama bottoms were soiled and her fingers dirty. The sickly sweet and rancid smell of decay pervaded the flat. She was fast losing her strength and her life.

I would flush away the black urine in the toilet basin. The cancer was not being treated and it was eating her up from inside. Lydia had a constant build-up of fluid on her lungs, which would be drained twice a week by the district nurses. It horrified her to see the amount of liquid that filled up the bottles each time. She referred to it as 'monstrous'. I think she secretly feared death by drowning from the fluid in her lungs as she refused to lie down in her bed, even though I had bought her special pillows to prop her up. She thought that the water she drank was somehow filling up her lungs or that there was a hole in her stomach which leaked water into her lungs. I don't believe that she ever really understood her illness at all and what it meant. Perhaps the cancer had affected her mind during this last stage or she was in too much shock.

One morning, she asked me if there had been a little girl playing in the living room the previous evening. She had heard the sounds of a child laughing. She described being aware of a little girl busily and feverishly drawing wonderful pictures by her side. I replied that, no, there hadn't been a child in the room. I imagined, that if there had been, perhaps it was this imagined little girl who had playfully drawn a thin red pencil line around Lydia's lips.

I realised, that during the quiet hours of the night, Lydia was visited upon by visions. Hazy companions merged with the dusky shadows in the room, dancing with the opioid-like effects of the medication before her failing sight.

The elixir

Although the medical team and palliative nurses did not make any home visits to assess Lydia's condition, due to Covid restrictions, I did speak to them by telephone and we had one video call. I described Lydia's struggle in the mornings, when she could barely move or speak a word. Lydia confirmed that she could hardly breathe during these episodes. The palliative nurse prescribed another drug, which I collected from the pharmacy as soon as it was available.

I would come to view this liquid medication as an elixir, laced with unknown, magic properties. I have already described the state Lydia was in first thing in the morning, as if she had been calcifying overnight, turning to stone and fossilising. One teaspoon of this potion and the effect was instantaneous. It was as if a magic spell had been cast to break a curse. Lydia described it as giving her a lovely warmth inside. Indeed, her eyes started to come alive once more and she was momentarily revived. A surge of energy ran through her, bringing her back from the clutches of the night and death. She was able to chat and even think about the possibility of washing herself. A beam of light briefly shining through a chink in the darkness. A moment of respite from the inevitable. The miracle of Hermione coming back from the dead in 'A Winter's Tale'. Stone turning to flesh once again.

Black scorpions

Not only were there snakes to contend with in the desert but scorpions too. When Lydia came face to face with her first scorpion, she climbed onto a chair and then a table. She managed to switch on the electric kettle and poured boiling water after the scurrying black creature as it scuttled away. During the early years, Guydon filled dishes with petrol and placed the foot of each bed leg in a dish to prevent the scorpions and beetles from climbing up onto the mattress. I think it worked, because Lydia never complained about scorpions in her bed!

Frustration

When Lydia was home during that intermission period of three weeks, the palliative team came on board from the local hospice (albeit remotely by video call, due to lockdown restrictions). They told me that we needed to start thinking about End of Life Care in order to explore the different options and find out what Lydia's wishes or preferences might be. However, Lydia would not entertain this in any shape or form. She simply didn't hear it. There was a wall. I couldn't get through to her. She skirted round the issue, avoided answering questions, ignored the crux of the matter and went off on a multitude of irrelevant tangents. I felt we were getting nowhere and that I was being left to drown. She seemed so wilful and stubborn, even obstructive. I felt she was acting selfishly and it exasperated me. I couldn't save her and she couldn't face the truth. There simply wasn't enough time for her to process and deal with the enormity of her situation and impending death. Things were moving so fast. She needed more time to reflect and understand. I felt that she was experiencing an existentialist crisis. She had always been naturally philosophical, introspective and analytical. She liked to ruminate over things slowly. But there was no time now. Practical decisions were required. I felt abandoned by her. Ironically, she was trying to stay with me by ignoring the reality and pain of her own situation. I think she believed that if we just stuck together then we could overcome all of the difficulties.

A white wedding?

Edzia made the journey in 1959 from London, to be present at her only daughter's wedding in Israel. At the time, it was not unusual for kibbutzim to make arrangements for a few marriages to take place at the same time in order to save on expenses. A rabbi would be called upon to make the proceedings legal, conducting the marriage ceremony within the kibbutz. Afterwards, a party would be organised for the happy couples!

However, for Edzia's sake, Guydon and Lydia agreed to conduct their ceremony in a more 'respectable' way. They had arranged for a simple wedding to take place at Beersheba (the main city in the Negev).

'Arranged' will give a misleading idea, perhaps. In fact, it was a rather hurriedly cobbled together affair, and not without its complications. Guydon had been reluctant to break off from his work in Faluja, insisting that it would be perfectly feasible for someone else to take his place at the ceremony. After all, it was just a formality! A friend could stand in for him and forge his signature at the registry office. What did he care for bourgeois niceties! My parents argued about it heatedly until, finally, Lydia convinced him that his idea was ludicrous and unreasonable. And apart from that, what would her mother think! No, this was a step too far! So, against his better judgement, my father finally agreed to turn up at his own wedding!

On the appointed day, the wedding party (consisting of four people) travelled to Beersheba on a dirt road in the kibbutz delivery truck. Harry drove with Edzia sitting next to him in the passenger seat. Sitting at the back of the truck on a sack of wheat was the bride, with the groom in between two milk churns! They had 60 kilometres to cover in open desert! The surface of the roads had been layered with salt from the Dead Sea. It was a bumpy ride, riddled with potholes that had been created by the cows licking the salt off the road's surface.

Edzia had purchased a lovely new blouse and skirt for Lydia to wear for the occasion as well as two wedding rings to be exchanged: a gold band for her future son in law and a simple gold ring mounted with a small pearl for Lydia. However, by the time they reached their destination, everyone was covered from top to toe in dirt and dust! Their clothes were crumpled and stuck to their skin. Everyone looked a little dishevelled and out of sorts. They smoothed down their creased clothes, shook the sand out of their hair and splashed their faces with water before entering the registrar's office. But no! Wait! There could be no wedding without two male witnesses who were unrelated to the couple! *'Hey! Anyone fancy a glass of free wine?'*. It didn't take long before two passers-by happily offered their services to help out the small wedding party.

Before a marriage ceremony can take place, the groom must agree to be bound by the terms of the 'ketubah' (marriage contract) in the presence of two witnesses. The 'ketubah' sets out the financial and marital obligations of the husband.

The marriage ceremony takes place under a 'Chuppah' (wedding canopy) which symbolises the new home being built by the couple when they become husband and wife. At the end of the ceremony, the groom breaks a glass, crushing it with his right foot and the guests shout, 'MAZOL TOV!'

Of course, in my parents' case, there were only four guests (two of which were complete strangers picked up from the street!)

During the marriage ceremony, the rabbi had given my mother a suspicious glance, as she was already a few months pregnant by then with her first child, my sister, Eldar.

The wedding party returned to Gvulot, where the newly married couple received a book from the kibbutz as a wedding gift: 'Marc Chagall, Dessins Pour La Bible' and moved into a little white house together.

And so began married life.

The smashed plate

One morning, Lydia smashed a plate in front of me. She was holding a little white side plate with some left-over toast on it. She threw it down on the floor in front of her and it broke into pieces. Then she tore off the emergency alarm that hung around her neck on a chord. This had replaced her mother's beautiful diamond pendant from Russia, which she never took off normally. However, in hospital, she had given the pendant to me for safe keeping before undergoing various tests, including chest x-rays. We both froze and stared at the broken plate on the floor. She was terribly upset. *I shouldn't be fighting with my daughter like this!* I reassured her that it was absolutely fine. I picked up the broken pieces of white pottery and toast. I told her that it would clear the air for both of us and that she should not be frightened by what had just occurred. I spoke to her softly, as a mother to a child. I told her that I was sorry. I was to blame. It was my fault and she should not worry. She looked sad and anxious and didn't say anything, staring at the air in front of her with a vacant, faraway look.

There were times when I felt Lydia and I were not synchronised and we seemed to jar against one another. I felt as if I were 'doing battle' with an obstinate child.

Something felt misaligned, like tectonic plates shifting uneasily beneath us, causing instability and uncertainty. There were rumblings of discord and displacement. The seismic landslide we both feared, yet could not openly talk about, was approaching at speed. There was a sense of heightened threat. What had always been at the core of our relationship (kinship, trust, closeness, a sense of understanding and being kindred spirits) seemed to be teetering on the edge of a precipice.

I had forgotten that feeling I had carried inside me throughout my childhood. She had been an absolutely wondrous creature to me, filling me with all of her loveliness and radiance. I had forgotten about helping her prepare the Passover meal every year, rolling the kneidlach for the chicken soup, whisking up egg whites to make macaroons and chocolate mousse for the almond cake. The pleasure of all of our long and deep conversations together and an intimately familiar, quiet and melancholic space we sometimes inhabited and felt comfortable sharing. All this seemed so far away now.

What I failed to understand, amongst so many things, was how little time we had left. One cannot imagine how final death is.

I too held back and turned away in order to keep the pain of losing her at bay and the contemplation of my own mortality at arm's length. We failed to meet (as we used so easily to do) during this most difficult of times.

There had always been a part of Lydia that existed in a remote place which only she had access to. At times, she seemed to be immersed in this private space, as if underwater, alone and far away. Or as if she were, once again, closed off from the world within the little partition with glass panelled doors that she had created for herself as a child in Brussels. Her absence would only last for a short time though; she would always resurface to reconnect and engage once again, a soft smile reappearing.

I found it difficult to reach out to Lydia during those last weeks of her life. She seemed to have drifted away; nothing was as it had once been.

The smashed pieces of pottery lying at her feet spoke of broken hearts and a life falling apart. We were both so sad, devastated, frightened, overwhelmed and lost. Time was running out more quickly than we could imagine as life ebbed away from her.

First born

Lydia and Guydon's first child would be born in Israel. When Lydia was close to giving birth, they had to drive to the nearest hospital some 60 kilometres away in the city of Beersheba, which could only be reached from Kibbutz Gvulot by taking a pot holed road riddled with dips and depressions. It was like travelling on the surface of the moon. Lydia believed that the bumpy ride may have helped the birth along! She was 23 years of age.

Lydia was taken to a hospital in the military barracks. There was no maternity ward as such. She found herself sharing a room with a group of expectant Bedouin mothers who were looking forward to their fifth or sixth child. Knowing it was Lydia's first, they gathered around her in a motherly and excited cluster, fussing and clucking over her. She was given all sorts of advice and told to drink sweet beer to bring on the milk. On the horizon, Lydia described seeing the women's husbands waiting for their wives with their camels. Perfectly still black silhouettes (like a child's paper cut-outs) standing patiently under the darkening orange-turquoise sky, casting long and elongated shadows across the distant plains.

After a fairly rapid and uncomplicated birth, a healthy baby girl was born to the delight of Lydia and Guydon.

After the birth of Eldar, my parents returned to Kibbutz Gvulot to a joyous reception. Babies were little treasures! Children were at the heart of kibbutz life. They were at the centre of the community, within which all dreams and hopes blossomed. They were the precious seedlings of the future: belonging as much (or more so) to the kibbutz as to the parents themselves.

The last few days

The night before I had to call the ambulance for the last time, I went to Lydia's flat to partially close the lounge curtains, switch on the night lights, prepare the medication, replenish the jug of water and offer Lydia some food. Everything was organised for the night ahead with essential items arranged in her tray within arm's reach. During the past few days, I had noticed that she was having trouble locating and getting hold of the things in her tray. She struggled to find and press the keys on the phone. She was not taking her medication. This night was even worse. Her fumbling hand seemed to swim inside the tray, pushing everything aside. I couldn't understand what was happening. It was as if she were dipping her hand into a goldfish bowl and the fish were giving her the slip each time she tried to grab one. Everything seemed to slide around, as if coated in oil slick. I had noticed that her co-ordination was beginning to be affected too. Sometimes she didn't quite align the spoon with her mouth. Other times, her trembling hands struggled to pour water directly into the glass. This had happened a few days earlier. She was clearly becoming weaker and less able with each passing day. I think she was also struggling to see at night, due to the macular degeneration, for which she had stopped receiving treatment. She was falling apart before my very eyes. Everything was unravelling like a bobbin of thread.

Rearing children in the kibbutz

After the initial happiness of bringing their new-born home to the kibbutz community, a new reality dawned. Mother and child were separated and made to live apart. Rules surrounding the rearing of babies and children were rigid and all youngsters were raised in line with the collective philosophy. There were different children's houses which catered for the different ages and stages of a child's development. The 'metapelet' was in charge of looking after all babies and children as a full- time nanny.

Eldar was placed in the babies' house with other recently born infants who were only a few days old. Babies and children were not brought up by their parents and nor did they live with them. The thinking behind this was to liberate women from a 'stifling' bourgeois upbringing and to spare children from the 'suffocating' influence of the mother so that they could grow up freely as true individuals, unfettered by the constraints of a traditional family unit. The system would allow mothers to return to work without delay (unencumbered by the need to care for their offspring full time) which would, in turn, facilitate their continued contribution to the kibbutz community and way of life.

Collective parenting was viewed as a means of establishing gender equality. Striving for equality of the sexes was intended to liberate women from solely domestic and child care duties. Communal child-rearing and education were seen as the first steps towards women's liberation. Communal children's houses were established to avoid parents' viewing their children as personal possessions, enabling the child to grow up as his or her own person. Emphasis was placed on fostering a child's sense of individuality, creativity and basic trust whilst at the same time preparing them to conform to collective life.

Children's houses were specially designed with age-appropriate facilities in mind, including: paddling pools, outdoor play pens, small gardens and play areas. Infants spent most of their time in these houses: eating, sleeping, growing, playing and learning together. Only during allocated afternoon hours would parents be permitted to collect their children and spend quality time with them, playing and doting on them for a few 'golden' hours every afternoon. Fathers were given the opportunity to bond with their children in a unique way, spending time with their child without the burden of financial or economic responsibilities and pressures, work commitments or long working hours.

The hope was that the relationships between children and their parents could become more moderate and harmonious. As discipline and education were shared responsibilities, the idea of an authoritarian father figure was eliminated. The intention of collective child-rearing was to veer away from patriarchal society and allow women to achieve social and economic liberation. The financial responsibility of the children was shared by the community which provided for all of their needs: education, child care, clothing, food and health care. Family was neither the main nor the only focus in the child's life. This broke with a cornerstone of traditional Jewish life: the focus on the nuclear family.

The expression of communal values was the bedrock of kibbutz society.

Today, however, an imposed separation between a mother and her new-born would certainly be viewed as unnatural and unacceptable (even shocking), as well as emotionally distressing for both mother and child. This approach to child-rearing was unique to the ideology of many kibbutzim at the time but no longer exists today. Furthermore, the 'idyllic' encounters between children and their parents did not allow for conflict to be experienced or worked through.

A *fateful morning*

The Saturday morning I discovered Lydia under the dining room table would seal her fate. The tray had toppled over and all of the contents were scattered on the carpet: medication, reading glasses, mobile phone, tissues. At first, I couldn't find her. Then I saw her, sitting under the table like a child hiding inside her den. She was half dressed. When I asked her what she was doing under the table, she replied that she had seen someone lying there (a man) whom she thought might be in some sort of trouble and needed her help. She must have shuffled her way towards him. She didn't understand why I was so concerned and perplexed. The whole situation seemed perfectly normal and reasonable to her. She was annoyed and impatient with me for expressing bewilderment.

Night shadows play tricks on our mind. Medication and illness induce visions and spectres. Lydia had seen Guydon hallucinating when he was terminally ill, filling her with fear and dread. He had been visited upon by dark, faceless figures looming over his hospital bed. The floor at the end of his bed had dipped and sagged like a soft drape in a Dali painting. Guydon had never feared these floating phantoms around his bed but rather viewed them as old friends. Lydia, on the other hand, was convinced that if she were ever to experience hallucinations, they would appear as malevolent and frightful presences. She was mistaken, however. Her visions would turn out to be quite harmless.

The paramedics arrive

When the paramedics arrived, they managed to lift Lydia out from her den under the dining room table. They sat her on a chair. After lots of questions and various examinations, they checked her mobility. Grabbing the Zimmer frame, Lydia pulled herself up and tried to take a step forward. But she couldn't. Her legs were buckling under her and the soles of her feet were sliding on the carpet as if she were skating on ice. Due to her impaired mobility, she had to be taken to the hospital for further examinations and supervision. However, she refused point blank. My heart sank. The paramedics sensed my desperation. They could not act without Lydia's consent. Finally, after much persuasion and a degree of coercion, she very reluctantly agreed to go with them to hospital. My heart lifted. I couldn't cope anymore.

Soon after her admission to hospital on this occasion (which would be her last) she deteriorated quickly and dramatically. She couldn't feed herself anymore or move from the bed. The nurses had to do everything for her. She was deeply distressed and said that she had lost all of her dignity. There was nothing left. Eventually she lost the ability to speak. I felt so responsible. I had the feeling that she thought she had been abandoned (yet again) to her fate; that I had forsaken and deserted her (like Edzia all those years ago during the war). I thought of the little child who had felt the separation from her mother as something cruelly imposed: like a cut, a deeply painful severance. Once again, she was left alone, terrified and silently enraged. It was overwhelming and beyond her understanding.

A Red Setter in Kibbutz Gvulot

Cori (a red setter) became the family pet and, like the children of the kibbutz, he roamed freely and independently wherever he pleased. His gorgeous red coat gleamed under the blazing sun as he bounded from one end of the kibbutz to the other, sniffing the ground as he went with his feathery tail held high. Cori had a brother, and between them, they had divided up the kibbutz into two sections. Woe betide the dog who trespassed into the other's domain! His brother was the stronger of the two and Cori would always come out the worse for wear after a fight. He would whimper and limp all the way home to my parents' little house, in a very sorry state, his tail in between his trembling legs. More often than not an ear would be slashed, his nose scarred, and deep toothmarks punctured his flanks and neck. Guydon would tend to his injuries, disinfecting and cleaning the blood from the cuts and gashes. Then, Cori would lie sleepily on the floor with his head resting on his paws and close his eyes, sighing deeply. A few days later, he would be off again, not having learned his lesson. Many more terrible fights would erupt between the two warring brothers which my father had to separate time and time again, getting in between their snapping, snarling teeth. Before the family left the kibbutz forever, my father found a good home for Cori.

The desert is their home

My parents grew to love their desert home with its endless expanse of sand, hot, dry winds, freezing, star-filled nights and silvery-red-ochre-coloured moons. It was not unusual for the temperature to plummet below zero at night time. Only three stones, one piled on top of the other, marked the border between Israel and the Sinai. One could unwittingly step over into enemy territory. All deserts are one, after all. It was a beautiful place. In the twilight, dusky moths gathered around the dim veranda light, bumping and brushing their wings against it. And so, my parents settled into the rhythms of this wild and untamed landscape far away from the cobbled and drizzly streets of Brussels.

First sighting of a Strawberry Moon

> A Strawberry Moon is a rare occurrence. This event marks the last full moon of the spring or the first full moon of the summer and represents a time of flux and change. The name originates from Native American tribes, specifically the Algonquin tribes, who used it to mark the beginning of the strawberry harvesting season. The sighting of the moon corresponded with the ripening of wild strawberries, acting as a natural indicator to gather and harvest the sweet fruit. The moon is not strawberry coloured at all, though. In fact, it is a striking orange and comes about when a full moon coincides with the summer solstice (when the sun is at its highest point in the sky), creating the longest day of the year and the shortest night. A Strawberry Moon rises above the clouds shortly after sunset, giving the sky a deep blue tone.

During Lydia's final stay in hospital, a Strawberry Moon appeared high in the sky one evening. I had never seen this before. I climbed the twisting, narrow stairs up to the attic of my house to get a better view. Why was it called strawberry, I asked myself? It was more like a glowing ball of warm, dark orange suspended in the dusky sky. I looked through the binoculars, trying to locate the 'Sea of Tranquillity'. I think I did. I saw mysterious patches and shadows. One could imagine all sorts of ghostly and fantastical creatures swimming silently and sinuously there, just below the opaque surface. Giant goldfish pushing and flexing through the eerie sea. Wispy, grey clouds, like slow cigarette smoke, drifted loosely around the orange ball.

When I went to see Lydia in hospital for the very last time, there were no machines in her little, yellow room. There was only a small plastic box under the sheet containing an ampoule of morphine which was steadily dripping into her blood stream, accompanying her on the last part of her journey to the end of her life. Drip... drip... drip... I imagined the opioid silently and stealthily flowing into her vein like a strange, meandering, purple mist, smothering the pain. Drip...drip...drip... The nurse comes in with a bunch of keys, unlocks the dispenser and changes the vial, carefully checking the small print first. She locks the box, punches in some numbers which light up electronically, making quiet beeping sounds, and deftly places it under the sheet again. Guydon had one of these boxes too, in hospital, under the sheets. Drip...drip...drip... She would fight on for another two days.

The medical team taking care of her at the end of her life were surprised that her heart just kept going, beating strongly. They had expected her to die sooner than she did. The cancer had overpowered her but she clung onto life for a few more days. That was just like her, she didn't give up. Only at the very end did she lose complete consciousness and slip away from us.

Night terrors

Guydon told me that, at some point, every child in the kibbutz suffered from night terrors. This was discussed repeatedly during the weekly committee meetings which took place in the communal dining hall in the evenings. Psychologists and experts were consulted. Everyone scratched their heads. No one had satisfactory answers or suggestions and they never found a way to eradicate the phenomenon of these night terrors. Perhaps the spine-chilling, midnight cries of the jackals invaded the children's troubled dreams, populating them with monstrous and screaming beasts. Parents were not there to comfort their children when they woke up in the middle of the night, tangled inside sweaty, twisted sheets in the darkness of the room. There were other adults to turn to, but the children didn't recognise them in the fog of their despair. Instead, they hid quietly under their tousled sheets, hardly daring to breathe, waiting for the first morning light to break.

First experience of motherhood

Life in the kibbutz for the children was, in many ways, wonderful and unique. But in other ways, it was flawed. The separation between mothers and their babies seemed to go against nature itself. Children's houses were designed to be practical and utilitarian. There were sleeping quarters, bathrooms and dining areas. Children grew up together, sharing everything. Much of their play was conducted outside or in their parents' houses which they could visit during allocated afternoon hours. Babies were bundled together in large outdoor play-pens in the shade whilst the 'metapelet' went about her duties.

As we already know, Eldar started life in the babies' house. Lydia struggled to breast feed her child who had difficulties latching on. The lack of privacy did not help matters either and Lydia felt under pressure. But surely this was the simplest and most natural thing to do? Truth be told, she had a miserable time with it. She remembered being called all through the night to feed her baby. She stumbled through the darkness holding a torch (the kibbutz was dimly lit with poor lighting), stepping over barbed wire, weaving around discarded farm equipment, trying to avoid ditches, praying that no stray bullet from the enemy beyond would reach her! Finally arriving in one piece at the baby house, she found the whole feeding experience daunting. She was expected to produce milk on demand and after such a perilous walk from her living quarters! Early bonding experiences were restricted. Lydia secretly yearned for time to stand still. Then she could have had all the time in the world to get close to her baby and know her. Alas, as soon as Lydia finished feeding her infant, she was surplus to requirements and made her way back to her separate accommodation. She must have had an aching desire to linger there all night long and watch her child fall asleep in her arms. These separations from her precious baby were very painful to her.

Kikuki

Guydon made up stories about a little creature called, Kikuki. He told these stories to the kibbutz children at bedtime or during lazy afternoons, stretched out on the grassy lawns or under the shade of the trees by the swimming pool with the Japanese bridge.

I imagine that he may have told the children a story that went something like this...

Kikuki is a creature from another world. He is easy to conjure up, as the star- studded night skies above Kibbutz Gvulot open up endless mysteries and possibilities for the imagination. He comes from the most dazzling star of all. Look! That very one up there, above your heads, the one that gleams the brightest. How does one describe this little creature who is like no other? Well, to start with, he has tufty black ears. His fine coat is patterned with the ravishing markings of an ocelot. He has the giant paws of an Indian tiger and the sinewy and elongated body of a serval. His tail (which is twice his body length) is covered in the thick, soft and luxuriant fur of a snow leopard. He has the hypnotic face of a lynx with citrine- coloured eyes shaped like diamonds. Unlike domestic cats, he does not meow. Instead, he has a low and rumbling purr which can, at times, be quite deafening! And let us not forget his little, white goatee beard.

Kikuki likes to keep himself in tip top condition! He is fastidious in his daily grooming, never missing a spot!

One night, he glides down from the brightest of all stars (whilst everyone in the kibbutz is fast asleep) like a flying fox, swishing his large tail from side to side. He scoops up some stars on his way which crackle on the tip of his tongue like popping candy.

In the morning, you will find evidence of his visits. Clues abound everywhere! You will discover unusual pawprints in the sand! He has sneaked into the children's house and stacked toys upon his nose like a performing seal at the circus, until they come crashing down on the floor! The 'metapelet' will arrive early in the morning to find a pile of broken and smashed bits! She will blame all of the children and give you a harsh telling off, making you tidy up and glue the pieces together before breakfast.

Next, Kikuki finds his way to the kibbutz kitchen, searching for his favourite snack: watermelon slices dipped in chilled milk! His wiry whiskers quiver with excitement and delight as they drip with milk, creating a pool on the kitchen floor! Crunching the slippery, flat, dark seeds between his sharp teeth is the best!

His eyes glint under the mirror moon with mischief! He goes on the rampage: trampling down fields full of golden wheat, leaving behind mysterious patterns and trails! Surely aliens have landed (the bewildered farmers muse) scratching their heads perplexedly.

He raids the peach and apricot orchards, leaving behind sticky pawprints. He pops the plump tomatoes growing on the vines like balloons with his needle-sharp claws, until all the seeds and pulp have burst out! He gorges on creamy avocadoes and chews on their large pips before discarding them on the pathways. Look out for big teeth marks! He tears up the pretty flower beds, searching for centipedes and beetles. He dips his huge tiger paw into the still, dark, silky water of the swimming pool, trying to catch hold of a rippling moon and his own reflection. He chases the chickens around the coop, making their feathers fly.

There is nothing Kikuki likes better than the smell of freshly laundered sheets and towels, especially if they happen to be a little damp! Can you imagine the mess he makes! Apricot, tomato and watermelon stains on the crisply pressed white sheets! The neatly folded piles of laundry in the airing cupboard tossed about and crumpled! Everything in disarray!

Eventually, after all these antics, he makes his way to the barn and flops down on a bale of hay in an exhausted heap, wrapping his long tail around himself like a feather eiderdown. He falls into a deep sleep whilst the cows eye him suspiciously. His tummy is as round as a barrel, heaving up and down.

Just before the first break of light he wakes up, arches his back and stretches (like all cats do), shaking out each paw, one by one. He yawns, sits and cleans his face with a paw, not forgetting to wash behind the ears! Then he enters the children's house and licks the forehead of each one of you with his warm, rough tongue which feels like sandpaper. His satiny tail brushes against each foot, slinking in and out and in between your beds. The sonorous rumble of his purr makes the furniture vibrate and tremble.

And just as you begin to stir, wiping the sticky damp from your faces and rubbing your tickled feet, Kikuki vanishes (as if he had never been) leaving a trail of havoc and mayhem in his wake...

Locusts

Sometimes, swarms of locusts would descend upon the kibbutz fields. The whole community, including the children, would get hold of pots and pans and metal spoons, banging them together to make one heck of a hullabaloo to scare the insects off. It felt almost biblical. The locusts seemed to materialise from the very air itself (millions upon millions of them) like a great white tidal wave, a sea mist, engulfing the land. My grandmother's story about the night her family pounded pots and pans together and smashed furniture in order to scare off the Cossacks comes to mind.

A beautiful time

They planted trees in the kibbutz to encourage little birds to come and live there. These birds would swoop in and out of the trees, busily looking for insects or suitable materials with which to build their nests. They flew over the swimming pool and, diving down, just clipped the surface of the water with their wings to scoop up a droplet of moisture in their tiny beaks. These small birds brought more life and music to the kibbutz.

One of the most appealing and distinctive aspects of kibbutz life for the children was the wonderful outdoor space they had to roam around in so happily and freely. The kibbutz was theirs to discover: a great outdoor adventure playground to explore with their peers. Kibbutz Gvulot was set within a stunning desert landscape, bordering the Sinai. Children grew up close to nature. Walking around in their little infant troops, young children became familiar with and grew close to this unique setting. They had access to the kibbutz gardens and play areas, the swimming pool, the farmyard and its animals. They walked around with a sense of freedom, confidence and independence, as children of the kibbutz. They experienced a sense of belonging and were treasured by the whole community. They were taught songs and the 'metapelet' made garlands of flowers to place upon their heads to celebrate Jewish festivals and holidays with an agricultural component like Sukkot and Shavuot, as well as Rosh Hashanah and Purim. Every child was treated equally. Birthday celebrations were simple affairs, with flowers, cakes, candles, songs and perhaps a little gift? A sense of collective responsibility held them. They walked under immense blue skies and glittering sunlight together, wearing their little sunhats.

The kibbutz swimming pool attracted butterflies and dragonflies to its lapping edges. At night, luminescent fireflies shone pools of oily iridescence onto the surface of the still, dark water. In the afternoons, children stood on their father's shoulders, tumbling, splashing and summersaulting into the water. There were screams of joy and excitement as children dived and jumped into the ripples of soft glassiness. Guydon had helped to build the swimming pool with the Japanese bridge, laying the blue mosaic tiles which reflected beneath the water. Paving stones were arranged around the swimming pool area. Grass lawns and trees providing shade were planted for the comfort of the community.

My parents wanted to be instrumental in creating a better world than the one they had emerged from, where the blood of millions had been so brutally and senselessly spilt. They worked hard to achieve this ideal. They had come to Kibbutz Gvulot with a vision, not a dream. They stayed for 10 years. However, that vision would eventually evaporate: a shattered dream, after all.

Cigarettes

During her illness, Lydia struggled to breathe due to severely impaired levels of oxygen. In order to stabilise her condition, she received a constant supply of oxygen from her hospital bed. This was on her first admittance. Once off the oxygen, she was put on a nebuliser. Finally, free from all tubes, she would suck in thin streams of air through clenched front teeth. This reminded me of the way she used to smoke. She had been a very heavy smoker for most of her life. Her preferred brand, 'Rothmans Royals' (extra- long, expensive, aristocratic looking cigarettes). Not a wisp of smoke escaped from her lips when she smoked. It was swallowed down deeply and disappeared without a trace. She bit into her cigarettes and the ashtrays overflowed with cigarette stubs indented with teeth marks. She smoked constantly and was rarely without a cigarette, either clenched between her teeth or balanced between her fingers. The slow, grey smoke tapered upwards; the ash smouldering at the tip, breaking off to fall onto the tablecloth or carpet.

In her seventies, she was diagnosed with Chronic Obstructive Pulmonary Disease. She was told, in no uncertain terms, that she would most likely end up on an oxygen tank for the rest of her life. She got scared and stopped smoking, literally, from one day to the next. But the cocktail of deadly toxins rolled up in those elegant looking cigarettes had already done their worst. At the age of 83, she was diagnosed with incurable lung cancer and died shortly after.

Lydia had smoked (ironically) as if her life depended upon it. She clung onto her 'Rothmans Royals' like an infant dangling onto its mother's nipple with bared teeth. She was fiercely defensive of her right to smoke. She bristled with irritation at any hint of criticism. She gulped down the smoke as if it were providing her with essential nourishment and nutrients. She interpreted censure from others as an attempt to curb her individual freedom and human rights! But there was more to it than that. The bitten cigarette ends and the compulsive smoking hinted at deep stresses and anxieties within her.

As a child, I would run my fingers over the embossed coat of arms on the front of the gold- edged, silky blue pack of 'Rothmans Royals' which promised *'extra quality'* and *'a super length, filter tipped cigarette'*. All that glitters is not gold, however. There was a constant smell of cigarette smoke at home during my childhood and the walls were nicotine stained. I swam through a fog of smoke, which I imagined could be sliced with a knife, like the thick and heavy tension I felt between my parents. A musty, acrid smell hung on our clothes.

A dreamy photograph

One photo stays with me. It is a close up of Lydia in the kibbutz swimming pool. She is smiling that beautiful, soft smile she had. She looks straight into the camera lens with warm eyes. Her thick, dark, curly, wet hair drips down her back; the water glistens and shimmers around her in a dreamy translucence. I can hear the sound of its faint lapping. The light has a lustre- like quality to it. Little shiny droplets cover her shoulders and arms like pearls. The Japanese bridge can be seen only faintly in the hazy background.

Sending the gift of a Strawberry Moon

As I studied that Strawberry Moon from the attic window, I wondered and indeed hoped, that Lydia might have seen it herself all those long years ago in the Negev. Perhaps a Strawberry Moon had appeared one night, over the sleeping kibbutz, as a luminous dark orange ball, suspended above the sleeping inhabitants. It bounced into the children's dreams in a shower of shooting stars and sparks, illuminating the indigo night with a shot of orange heat.

Hovering above the kibbutz, an orange disc is enveloped by greyish-blue swirls of mist. As if touched by the light strokes of a painter's brush or the slow and sinuous coils of cigarette smoke, twisting out into the form of spreading branches. Just like when Lydia and Guydon smoked endless cigarettes together. Rings of smoke would interlock and intertwine or, perhaps, strangle?

Peering at the Strawberry Moon through the binoculars, I imagined stretching out my arm to capture it in the palm of my hand. I would blow it in Lydia's direction, just like she used to blow me kisses. It would float towards her, passing through hospital walls and corridors like a spectre trying to reach her. It would hover over her silvery hair. She would sense its warm glow upon her closed shell-like eyelids and lips. Her breaths are shallow but she gently breathes in the orange globe. It enters her, settling and calming her. It gives her comfort and, finally, she begins to let go.

A picnic under the shade of the eucalyptus trees later on...

After I was born in 1965, the family were no longer living in the kibbutz but remained in Israel for a few short years thereafter. We would enjoy little picnics under the dappled shade of the eucalyptus trees, as a little family unit. There were small wooden stools and tables, shaped like overgrown toadstools in the forest. The ground was littered with dry, blackened leaves, like discarded, old banana skins. A wicker basket was packed with napkins, fresh, crusty, bread, hard boiled eggs, cheese, sliced cucumber and tomatoes, fresh watermelon and pomegranates. Eucalyptus trees are fast-growing evergreens, well adapted to extreme heat. The long, dark-green and blue leaves point downwards towards the earth. If you crush them between your fingers, the oils within the leaves are released, giving off a medicinal scent. If you cup your hands to your face, you can breathe in the peppermint-like perfume. The trees have flowers too, creamy- white, yellow, pink and red, dangling like fancy tassels from a haberdashery. The dead outer layer of bark sheds smooth ribbons. Underneath, new bark emerges, ranging in colour from blue, purple, orange and maroon. Sometimes, a red resin seeps from the breaks in the bark, like blood.

Last words

Only at the very end, just a few days from taking in her last breath, did Lydia come back to me. I had called the hospital to speak to her. It took them a while to locate her, as she had been moved to the little yellow room. The phone must have been placed next to her ear on the pillow. I don't think she had any strength left and would not have been able to hold the phone in her hand. She repeated my name in a calm, clear and familiar voice and then said:

It's ok, it's ok. I'm not far now…

The phone fell away from her. Those last words tumbled out like rose petals or confetti. Anger and despair had left her. She understood and accepted her situation, wanting me to know her good feeling for me and that she was taking care of things.

I went to see her for the final time, shortly after this. But by then, her eyes were closed and she could no longer speak to me.

She came back to me at the very end. She had found herself once again. Her lips were brushed by the warm glow of a Strawberry Moon, after all, sent to her on a gentle spring breeze. She had reached out to me with her dying breath to give me a few last words of comfort. There was peace between us once more as our minds met for the last time. We had not forsaken one another. For this, I will be forever grateful to her. She left me with a warm, golden glow as she slipped away and said goodbye, understanding that I had not deserted her, after all. Each plate of armour began to fall away from her and melt into rivulets of molten gold.

Hospital trays

The trays on hospital wards can be wheeled around and adjusted (up or down) to fit over the beds. For Guydon, this tray would become his world during those long weeks of being marooned in hospital towards the end of his life. He liked everything to be organised just so. He was very meticulous about it. He focused on this arrangement, particularly at the end of the day, in preparation for the night ahead before we left. It was all very orderly: pills in small paper cups, a box of tissues, fruit, a little notepad and pen, a jug of water, his mobile phone, extra bottled drinks, a newspaper or book. Everything must have its place.

At the end of her life, Lydia's hospital tray was empty and wiped clean. There was nothing on its surface, not even a jug of water. So this is how we leave this world, I thought. The room was bare and quiet. Just those lemon painted walls and the feel of a warm and gentle breeze from the opened window. The stiff, blue pleated curtains shifting slightly. I thought about her books at home and the work that she had been in the midst of preparing for her French literature class. Some notes in blue ink written in her very distinctive cursive script, left on the dining room table.

After everything (a whole life, with all of its joys and struggles, trials and tribulations) there she was in her hospital gown, all alone in a plain little room with a bed, an empty tray and a chair for me to sit on, nothing more. The quiet was only interrupted by her spasmodic groans and the nurse's visits. Her eyes were closed. She was slipping away whilst fighting to stay here, on this earth, with us.

Only a few weeks before this moment she had said that she did not fear death but didn't know how she would get there. I think the answer is that we (more often than not) have no choice in how we get there, it just happens and there is much we cannot know, imagine or do about it.

Death had crept into her life and she turned her face away from him in disgust. He hunched over her shoulder, breathing his foul stench down her neck, waiting to spring into action and take her. She had resisted and ignored him. She turned the other way and refused to look at him. But he was patient and waited by her side for as long as it took, in the shadows and unyielding. He is not put off by people turning away from him. His grip remains firm and he does not let go. He was steadily reeling her in, like bait on the end of his hook. Death is inevitable, yet unthinkable. But she would not be snatched by him without a fight. He would need to prise her roots away from the rich earth within which they were so deeply embedded.

Guydon describes a typical day on the kibbutz

You woke up very early in the morning to start your day's work in the fields. I made my first cup of coffee on the little gas stove in our room. I stepped out onto the small patio and sipped the strong, sweetened black coffee whilst surveying my little garden of wonders. The flowers and plants looked fresh from the previous night's watering. Indeed, it was chilly at that time in the morning as the kibbutz was quietly stirring. I gave the plants one last showering and replenished the water in the tin basins for the little birds, before heading off in the jeep to work in the fields. The sky was like an ever- changing picture, daubed and stained with vibrant streaks of red, crimson and orange at first. Then slowly changing into purples and violets which eventually faded as the blue skies of the day emerged. After a couple of hours work in the fields (having taken advantage of the cool, early morning) I would head to the communal dining hall to have breakfast: sour cream, cold meats, vegetables, boiled eggs, bread and marmalade. I went back to the fields and worked through till noon, returning to the communal dining hall for a cooked meal with meat or fish, potatoes, salad and rice. It would be far too hot to work after lunch, so we took a two- hour siesta. I then went back to the fields in the afternoon for a couple of hours before finishing my day's work. I would come home to shower off the dirt and sweat. The hot water was heated by a very primitive looking contraption. But it did the job. And how I enjoyed the shower! Then I could relax. We collected our children from their houses, spending lots of quality time with them, playing and swimming. I had no worries and no pressures to deal with. Kibbutz life suited me well. It was a simple, well organised and uncomplicated life. After several hours in the company of our children (after which we would drop them off at their children's house for the night), we made our way to the communal dining hall for the evening meal. Then there was a long evening to look forward to. There were weekly committee meetings where everything was discussed and voted on democratically. The rest of the time was yours to do as you pleased: rest, read, write, chat, play chess, listen to music, enjoy an espresso at the club house or watch a film.

Kibbutz society was not so unlike other societies. There were plenty of petty disputes and disagreements between members, just as you would find anywhere else. On one occasion, I ended up by slapping one of the members across the cheek over a dispute concerning a kettle! There was no reason on earth for this idiot to refuse my simple request for a kettle to be made available to my mother- in- law whilst visiting us as our guest in the kibbutz. Edzia was travelling all the way from London and I wanted her to be as comfortable as possible during her stay. I understood how important having the facility to make her own coffee would be for her! A small request, surely! But this imbecile refused us the kettle and insisted the matter be brought up at a committee meeting and voted on! I had no patience for these stupid situations! So I slapped him and he quickly provided us with the kettle, no questions asked!

Kibbutz life fitted Guydon like a glove and he embraced it fully. He did not experience a sense of hardship there, quite the opposite. He was free. He adapted and made the desert his home. He had arrived as a very idealistic young man. He would become a husband and father within that unique setting. I think it is fair to say that, in many ways, he flourished there and was in his element. Like the rarely flowering cactus plant, it would be a short-lived period in his life, where he found stability and fulfilment. I would say that it brought out the best in him and kept him on the straight and narrow. Collective life required conformity and discipline. The kibbutz was a place of 'containment' which succeeded in keeping Guydon's more chaotic and impulsive side in check. He went along with the natural and reassuringly predictable rhythms of the life he found there, deeply contented.

Dinner with Ben Gurion

Once Lydia was established in Kibbutz Gvulot, she was given the opportunity to visit other kibbutzim around Israel. One of these was kibbutz Sde Boker, also in the Negev, where David Ben Gurion joined the visitors for the evening meal. Although he was Prime Minister (Israel's first), he still resided on the kibbutz. After the meal, he stepped into the kitchen to wash the dishes. He was on kitchen duty that week. This illustrated the egalitarian principles upon which all kibbutzim were founded. Everyone belonging to the community had to do their bit and there were never any exceptions to the rule. Rotas and work schedules were shared out equally amongst the members, no matter who you were.

Ilia and the kibbutz

Ilia's separation from Edzia some years after the war, hit him hard and left him at a loss and in despair. He fell into a profound depression after she left him and attempted to take his own life. However, she simply couldn't carry on anymore. She had come to the end of the road: she had no strength left and could not continue as before. The children (Harry and Lydia) were in Israel, leading their own lives now. She had done her best to find a way forward with Ilia, on different terms. However, after two years of trying, she realised that she was at a dead end. He would not change his ways. He had always shirked from his financial responsibilities towards her and the family. He remained obstinately work shy and perfectly happy to let Edzia carry the load. But she no longer had the strength or will to continue in the same way. She eventually pleaded for a divorce. Ilia turned down her request initially. He would not hear of it. He got down on his knees and begged her not to leave him, tears streaming down his face. He had always been so completely dependent on Edzia and had absolutely no means of supporting himself, having relied on her for everything. He had never imagined a future without her and had taken her for granted. Edzia, on the other hand, had courage. The prospect of leaving Ilia did fill her with fear and uncertainty; she was not wholly sure that it would be the right thing to do. But she was not afraid of being on her own. She had always been the breadwinner and had confidence in her ability to take care of herself financially. Her fears and hesitation were based more on a feeling of guilt. How would Ilia manage without her? Was she throwing away her marriage? All those years of being with someone! They had survived the war together. On the other hand, how could she go on in the same way? It was impossible.

Finally, Ilia agreed to a divorce and it was arranged that he would join my parents in Israel and live with them on kibbutz Gvulot. I believe Edzia had been instrumental in making this possible. She had been fearful for his state of mind. She could not move on with her life (as she so desperately wanted to) before being assured that Ilia was going to be alright. Eventually, she was free to re-marry and moved to London to share a life with Benny, an English cousin whose parents, Jacob and Sheindle Goldbrum, had been born in the small Polish town of Wodzislaw before emigrating to London somewhere between 1913 to 14. Benny had always harboured a secret love for Edzia. After liberation, he was stationed in Belgium with the British army. He asked for leave to find Edzia, not knowing whether she had survived. He made his way directly to Rue Marie Christine, where he found her. And the rest, as they say, is history.

But is it? And although I am sorely tempted to leave Edzia's story there, things did not turn out to be quite so simple. Benny was a successful businessman in London when Edzia married him. He was in the rag trade and then went on to purchase two hotels in Kings Cross. Edzia enjoyed a life of comfort for many years. Benny forbade her to lift a finger or ever work again. When he retired, he sold off all of his businesses and the couple looked forward to a secure and well- earned retirement. But Benny had been a life- long gambler and a regular client of many a London casino (losing eye watering amounts of money over the years). However, as long as he had an income from his businesses, the losses could be sustained. At some point after he retired, Benny had one final, mad fling at the roulette wheel and lost everything! Poor Edzia! Yet again, she would be faced with catastrophe. This time, during the latter part of her life and so unexpectedly! They ended up having to manage on a modest income and once again, my grandmother had to take control.

Ilia became a big part of my parents' lives after he joined them on their kibbutz. They grew close. And although he was more accustomed to living in a city, Ilia adapted to a simple way of life. Everything was taken care of by the kibbutz community and he settled in with his family close by.

He was in the habit of feeding the kid goats with bottles of milk. They followed him around the kibbutz everywhere. The children gathered around him excitedly as he held the little creatures in his arms. He would play chess in the evenings with Guydon. Apparently, he cheated often! Nonetheless, Guydon let him win with his usual good humour! There would be many political arguments. He did not agree with the left- wing politics of the Mapam Party as it stood at the time. He had come as an outsider and was a critical observer of the kibbutz and much of the left- wing ideology it was founded upon. My parents remained staunchly committed to left wing politics in Israel during that period.

However, he stayed on after the family left for a new and independent life beyond the parameters of the kibbutz. It was a natural and easy decision for him to remain behind. He considered the kibbutz his home. He took his meals in the communal dining area, enjoyed the pretty gardens, spent time reading books and newspapers, wrote letters, made coffee or tea in his little room, gave the children sweets and biscuits, discussed politics and current affairs with other members, visited his family in Jerusalem and Tel Aviv and continued to involve himself with Zionist matters. Later on, he learned a little English so that he could read my letters and write back to me (this was when we had moved to London). We visited him a few times and he came to London on several occasions also. I remember him as a kind, gentle, affectionate grandfather. He had soft hands. I didn't know him very well and we spoke different languages, which I regretted.

Edzia and Ilia at an evening dinner dance, post war Brussels

Edzia and Benny- happily married for many years in London until Benny's final act of wrecklesness changed their lives

Kibbutz society

Children were at the centre of kibbutz life. Kibbutz society was designed to allow for only 'golden' experiences between parents and their children (during those precious afternoon hours) leaving no place for discord or conflict to be experienced or worked through. Thus, a multitude of feelings would not have been acknowledged or expressed. The utopic vision of the kibbutz (however well intentioned) possessed elements of fantasy which did not stand up to reality. Handing over her first born to the collective community caused Lydia feelings of deep regret. However, adherence to the kibbutz way of childrearing was accepted and remained unchallenged at the time, although it clearly went against natural instincts and desires and was not in the best interests of the mother or child. Furthermore, children grew up not really knowing their parents intimately.

The hope was that the relationships between children and their parents could become more moderate and harmonious. Discipline was a shared responsibility and the financial responsibility of the children was also shared by the community which provided for all of their needs. This collective approach to child-rearing veered away from the patriarchal model and the father's authority. Children were not dependent on their fathers economically, socially, legally or otherwise. Fathers were given the opportunity to bond with their children through quality time: much more so than in a non- kibbutz environment, where work commitments and long hours might interfere with family life.

Families had no financial responsibility whatsoever as the kibbutz took care of its members' economic affairs. By shifting the responsibility from the family to the community at large, the theory was that women could achieve greater gender equality without hindering their role as mothers. Laundry and cooking duties were done communally. Women worked alongside men in the fields, sharing heavy, manual labour. This was a common feature of many utopian communities.

However, in reality, women seemed to gravitate towards the more traditional roles, such as child care, working in the kitchens and laundry rooms. This is what seemed to be occurring in Gvulot, at least. Apart from picking tomatoes for a short period, Lydia looked after the children and also prepared meals for the community. Married women were encouraged to knit sweaters for their husbands and were allocated yarns of wool, knitting needles and simple patterns to follow. This did not appeal to Lydia in the least! Apart from which, she wouldn't know where to start! So she made an arrangement with a friend to cover her work duties whilst she knitted Guydon a cardigan! There were many aspects to kibbutz life that she found limiting and narrow, especially as an intelligent, young woman.

Kibbutz Gvulot was founded on a combination of socialist and Zionist doctrine. There was disdain for orthodox Judaism but a desire for the community to have non- religious Jewish characteristics. Jewish religious practices were banned. All forms of private ownership were scorned upon and kibbutz members enjoyed few personal possessions.

Many kibbutzim, like Gvulot, were established in remote parts of the country for strategic reasons and to define borders. Kibbutz members found immense gratification in bringing land back to life by planting trees and making the land productive. Kibbutzim saw themselves as 'making the desert bloom'. A strong work ethic was essential and held in the highest regard. Members hoped to be more than farmers: they wanted to be instrumental in creating a society where all would be equal and free from exploitation.

Kibbutzim were strict societies with a clearly defined ideology and rules. Transgressions would be communally frowned upon. Collective life required conformity and discipline. The expression of communal values was the bedrock of kibbutz society. Marriage was regarded as an expression of exclusivity, therefore communal weddings were organised and couples were discouraged from sitting together in the communal dining hall, for example. I think Lydia was totally unprepared for this aspect of communal life, it did not exactly fulfil her more romantic dreams at that time.

These small and isolated communities were subject to petty, everyday disputes and disagreements. Every single decision would need to be approved collectively during weekly meetings. Kibbutzim could be places of gossip, exacerbated by a lack of privacy, the regimentation of work and leisure schedules. But they also had a reputation for being culture- friendly: nurturing the arts, producing writers and artists.

The Kibbutz Years, 1950's

Guydon- early years in the kibbutz

The Negev

Lydia- newest member of kibbutz Gvulot

Guydon- farming in the desert

Lydia and the kibbutz swimming pool

The beauty of the desert that surrounded them

Little visitors on the patio wall

The start of family life: Guydon and Lydia with their first born child, Eldar, 1959

What has Cori found in the desert?

Ilia with a kid goat and some little admirers!

Harry, the kibbutz truck driver

Guydon's flowering cactus-a mysterious underwater creature

Part 5 Retrospective Reflections

The dream, from Lydia's perspective

Lydia said the desert was very beautiful with a timeless quality, seeming to go on forever. You either loved it or disliked it. And she certainly didn't dislike it.

Both her and Guydon had joined a young kibbutz, at its early stages of development, founded upon the principles of equality and shared labour.

It had been an immense achievement to be able to cultivate and grow crops in the desert; to create gardens where trees, shrubs and flowers flourished, attracting little birds. They created a whole new ecology, within which a community was able to subsist and thrive. This moved and touched her deeply.

Lydia grew to develop a strong bond with her surroundings. The landscape that enveloped them was powerful and could not be ignored. It stirred strong feelings, one way or another. She did not feel a connection with Israel, as such. It was more the life they had created for themselves on a frontier kibbutz in the middle of the desert, her marriage to Guydon and their first child together in such a unique setting.

They had begun their lives in Israel, following their socialist principles. They possessed strong political convictions and believed that the only hope for peace was to share the land and country with their Palestinian neighbours. They recognised the might of the Arab world that surrounded them. The only way forward was to achieve peace.

This was part of their dream. They had chosen to experience life in a very different way from that of their parents, by becoming pioneers and leaving everything behind them.

A vision for the future

After the 'ashes' of the Holocaust, Lydia and Guydon returned to the safety of their families. How fortunate they were! Their parents had survived, against all the odds! Soon, they would join 'Hashomer Hatzair' which was to become an increasingly important part of their lives as they grew up in post war Brussels. Their involvement and commitment became ever more serious and intense. I came across lots of photographs of the youths from their group: camping out in large fields, putting up tents, building fires, participating in exercise drills and sports events, fooling around like youngsters do, walking together through the streets of Brussels, arms linked. It was clear to see (through these snapshots) the profound sense of camaraderie and connection between these youngsters, whose families had all suffered horrifically at the hands of the Nazis.

Guydon with a group of girls from the youth movement, Brussels, 1950

The movement took over their lives. Preparation to make 'Aliyah' (Jewish emigration to Palestine) was well on its way. By the time they were young adults, they had made up their minds to go to Israel to be part of the socialist vision, rather than pursue their studies at university and forge professional careers for themselves. Guydon departed before Lydia, travelling from the port of Marseille all the way to Haifa. It took him several weeks to get there by ship. She would follow on, two years later. During this time lapse, they would write many letters to each other: exchanging philosophical and political ideas, discussing literature and music, expressing romantic sentiments.

Much later on in their lives, they would look back on this period and seriously question the wisdom of their decision to leave Brussels in pursuit of an ideal which was doomed from its very inception and for which great sacrifices were made.

Passion and indoctrination

Guydon threw himself into the youth movement, Hashomer Hatzair, body and soul. The movement captured his imagination and seemed to offer everything he could possibly dream of. He joined as a young teenager. Soon his future would be mapped out and shaped by an ideology that appealed to him on so many levels. His objective would be to become part of the 'Halutzim' vision: to set out for Israel as a heroic pioneer, join a settlement and cultivate the land for the future development of the country. The idea of bringing land back to life by making it productive was immensely appealing, thus 'making the desert bloom'.

Envoys from Mapam (a left-wing political party in Israel) were sent to Hashomer Hatzair youth groups all over Europe in order to entice youngsters to join their cause and be instrumental in their vision of building a socialist state in Israel. They believed that kibbutzim could be the cells from which the right spirit would emanate and spread throughout the whole country. Theirs was a utopic vision.

Guydon became totally engulfed in the movement. It seemed to fulfil all of his needs and aspirations. It offered him a context in which to express all of his ideas for the future. It offered him excitement, adventure and happiness. These were fulfilling years for him. A golden time. He immersed himself in its atmosphere and flourished. He felt on top of the world. Anything could be achieved. He was very socially involved with like-minded youths and sweet, innocent romances blossomed. Hashomer Hatzair was founded upon strong principles, among them: no smoking, no modern dances and no casual sex. How closely these principles were followed, I cannot say for certain.

He invited members back to his home in Rue de la Poterie for meetings and discussions in his small bedroom, where he stoked up the fireplace with coal. His young guests stretched their hands out to feel the heat emanating from the glowing fire which soon warmed up the room. On one occasion, his little brother, Daniel, interrupted one of these gatherings by placing his potty in the middle of the room to relieve himself in front of the crowd! What a performance! Guydon was annoyed and had to clean up the mess! But he loved his little brother all the same. He often picked Daniel up from school, holding his hand all the way home. Later on, when he had emigrated to Israel, Guydon would regularly send Daniel stamps for his collection.

However, looking back on this intense period, Guydon believed that they had been indoctrinated, even brain-washed by the movement and its representatives. And although he had experienced being part of the movement as one of the high points of his life, he recognised that he had thrown away the opportunity to study and shape a long-term, solid future for himself.

Whilst still a school boy in Brussels, he had been selected for a scholarship for gifted students. But he turned it down, preferring to dedicate himself to the movement. Nothing his parents said could dissuade him. At the age of 16, he was offered a place on a seminar in Jerusalem to study Hebrew, Jewish history and culture for one year.

He jumped at the chance and packed in his school studies for good! When Guydon returned to Brussels, he was invited to become a youth leader for the movement. Shortly after this, he made the final commitment to join other pioneers (known as 'halutzim') and underwent a year of training before setting off to establish a modern, self-sustaining, agricultural settlement in the Negev desert.

The socialist vision for the State of Israel never came to fruition. In fact, Lydia and Guydon would witness the country's steady and catastrophic shift towards the far right over time, killing off any hope for peace.

Later on in life, Guydon was of the opinion that his ten years on a kibbutz had been for nothing and been wasted; it had been an illusion. However, there is no doubt that they had also been some of the best and most formative years of his life, very much shaping him as a man and human being.

Deeper questioning

In some ways, Lydia also felt that they had been exploited by Hashomer Hatzair and Mapam. They were a young, impressionable and vulnerable group, emerging from a time of brutal persecution. And in their pursuit of a dream to latch onto, many personal elements were overlooked. Deeper questions were not asked or explored. They threw themselves into the movement with political naivety. They were a confused generation to begin with, having survived such horrors. The movement seemed to provide them with all of the answers and absolute certainty: a belief that they would be able to change society and build a new future for themselves. But how can you do this without first knowing who you are? This is the question Lydia posed. In this, they failed. Something was missing and incomplete. They were duped by a utopic vision which was fundamentally flawed.

Guydon had found the political dialectic of Hashomer Hatzair intellectually satisfying and exciting. He never questioned it.

It fulfilled all of his desires at the time and gave him a clear direction for his future life. He had believed in it wholeheartedly.

They were searching for a way in which they could re-define the world. They were seeking a new identity and place within the world that would enable change to take place. They sought to shape a world of greater justice, equality and humanity.

In some ways they achieved and lived this, in other ways the utopic vision failed and seemed to collapse. Most of the people from their original group did not stay on and eventually left the kibbutz.

Lydia and Guydon

There is so much one could write about my parents' marriage. But that remains their private story. It could be said that they had a disastrous marriage and yet they were inseparable.

They came from the same place and the same experience. Nothing could sever this connection between them. In fact, it bound them together (no matter what).

Guydon suffered from a type of self-imposed amnesia. He had a bad memory, generally speaking. There were large gaps from his past that he could not fill. He had erased memories, experiences, episodes. Or they had simply faded over time.

Sometimes his memories were confused, blurred or mixed up. It took a great deal of perseverance and coaxing, on my part, to prise any information out of him. He was obliging enough to comply, albeit against his better judgement and will at times!

He didn't seem to enjoy talking about his past. At first, he was resistant, impatient and irritated. But I would not give up and, together with my mother, we would encourage him to think back and remember. Eventually, he began to relax and experience the pleasure of recollection.

'Your mother is my memory...'

He would often say this during these conversations of reminiscing. It is true, my mother remembered events from her own past in great detail as well as events from Guydon's past which he had forgotten.

Their marriage was quite broken and yet they had shared the deepest of experiences together. They had been children of the war, emerging from hidden places, returning home to hear stories of tragedy, horror and annihilation. They had been the lucky ones. History had brought them together at a certain point in time and they had made their own history together. Their marriage was complex and tortured. Elements of pain were part and parcel of their love story.

Lydia was haunted by the question of 'saving the children'. She challenged the idea that it had been the best and only option during the Holocaust for Jewish families (like her own and Guydon's) to send their children away into hiding with complete strangers. What if they were mistreated or abused? What if they survived the war, only to find themselves orphaned and alone? Should a life be saved at all costs? She was strongly of the opinion that a small child would be better off taking its chances with its parents rather than being abandoned to the unknown.

Guydon understood Lydia's moral/ philosophical dilemma on this subject. But from his point of view, it was simply a matter of making a decision. You either did or you didn't send your child away. The desire to survive is a strong human instinct. He found Lydia's viewpoint quite unusual, unconventional and even extreme.

He admired Edzia, saying that she had been a remarkable woman who had faced all the difficulties of life head on. She had not hesitated in bringing Lydia back from the first hiding place, at great personal risk to herself and her child. They could have been stopped by the Germans at any point, arrested or even shot.

He felt that Lydia still felt like an abandoned child and that her attitude reflected her own personal struggle with the past.

They asked themselves, was it possible for parents (like Moishe and Mariem) to come to terms with the death of a child who had been murdered at the hands of the Nazis?

There were periods in their marriage, when the anger and hurt between Lydia and Guydon was so intense that they did not communicate. There was an imposed silence between them.

From my childhood memories, I remember the hand written notes and cash left on the kitchen table from my father in the mornings, before he headed out to work in the taxi for the day. The words went something like:

> *Money for bills and shopping...*
> *I will be back late...*

Sad, lonely notes, revealing the chasm between them.

But on some occasions, they would enter into deep and philosophical conversations or reminisce, as previously described.

Other times, they would remember French and Hebrew songs from an earlier life which had shaped and bound them together in so many ways. During these moments they were one: united, synchronised and joyful.

Special meals would also bring them together to celebrate family birthdays, Pesach or Rosh Hashana. There was never a religious component to these Jewish festivities. It was about gathering the family members together, creating memories and enjoying delicious food and mouth- watering homemade desserts.

After Lydia's death on 17th April 2020, Daniel recollected that she had possessed the most exquisite voice when she sang to his group from Hashomer Hatzair, as they gathered around camp fires in the evenings during trips to the Ardennes. She had been his 'madricha' (youth supervisor) and was put in charge of various groups of younger children. Daniel had not forgotten the smooth and dulcet, mellow notes she had sung which seemed to float on the night air, mingling with the sparks, crackle and flickering flames of the camp fire.

Part 6 Leaving Kibbutz Gvulot

After a period of ten years, the decision to leave the kibbutz was finally made. My parents had first arrived as pioneers, motivated by ideology and strong political convictions. They had wanted to live in a different way from their parents' generation. They believed it was possible to shape this vision in the middle of the Judean desert. The challenges they faced made them even more determined in their resolve. They were living a life according to their ideals and deeply held principles. It was a unique and 'romantic' time, when it seemed possible to turn dreams into concrete realities. They were respected for choosing a difficult path. Their commitment was acknowledged, if not wholly approved of by all.

Guydon adapted to kibbutz life and to his new environment easily. It was not so much the ideology (which had brought him there in the first place) as the feeling of freedom from the 'materialistic' world and conventional expectations that had appealed to him. The idea of working collectively for a common goal was an attractive proposition at this point. There was a feeling of profound achievement, but not in the sense of an individual career or personal gain. Reaping the rewards from working the land successfully for the good of the community (in order for their way of life to be viable and sustainable) was extremely fulfilling and satisfying. Making this kind of contribution was profoundly meaningful to him and matched his general philosophy at the time.

However, after ten years, many of their common dreams had evaporated. And when a new opportunity presented itself, Lydia and Guydon looked forward to shaping a different future for themselves. Most of their close friends had already left, establishing new and independent lives for their families beyond the parameters of the kibbutz.

Leaving the kibbutz was not a straightforward process. You were obliged to give an in-depth explanation for your decision in front of the General Assembly. It was a painful and difficult course of action to take. The kibbutz was very reluctant to let its members go. They were viewed as traitors who were betraying the cause.

My parents' contribution to kibbutz life had been considerable, yet there was no remuneration for ten years of hard work, sacrifice and commitment. In fact, they left with less than they had arrived with all those years ago, as idealistic youngsters. Now they were married and had a young child to raise and take care of. They were given nothing to start their new life outside the kibbutz with. They left with one suitcase, containing all the possessions they had in the world: some French novels, the Chagall book which they had received as a wedding gift from the kibbutz and a few items of clothing. The system seemed harsh and punitive. Together with the pain of leaving, there was also a bitter aftertaste.

And although Guydon had been very comfortable with most aspects of kibbutz life (easily adapting and making it his home) after ten years, he too looked forward to change, a new adventure and challenge. He did not object to their leaving.

Lydia yearned to have a second child born outside the collective system. She felt that her first born had belonged to the kibbutz and not to her. She wanted to experience a more conventional family life, living in her own home where she could look after the children herself. She wanted the freedom to make her own decisions, without the constraints of petty regulations and rules. She dreamt of doing something as simple as choosing clothes for her children!

However, the flip side of this was that the kibbutz had provided them with absolute security. There were no financial worries or concerns. Leaving felt like entering the unknown. This meant that it was not a straightforward decision and Lydia felt somewhat conflicted about it.

It is true to say that the kibbutz had 'held' Lydia and Guydon for ten years during their early life together as a young couple. Going out into the wider world was, in many ways, a daunting prospect. They had no real experience of life beyond the kibbutz, where family life was so different and they would inevitably be faced with many challenges.

They would be swerving away from the fundamental philosophy and principles of kibbutz life, whereby all notions of private property and ownership were scorned upon. One worked for the good of the 'collective' and not for individual gain or subsistence. They had been removed from the everyday economic struggles and realities of life. They were naïve in this respect, perhaps.

In many ways, I feel that they were unprepared for the challenges that lay ahead. Individual freedom comes with economic responsibility. They would have to become self-reliant and make every single decision for themselves. Free will comes with a different kind of obligation and accountability. Their aspiration, up until then, had been to fulfil a particular political and ideological vision. They were ill- equipped to deal with many aspects of the outside world, which were unknown to them. They had been shaped differently, which gave them wonderful and unique attributes but also put them at a disadvantage and made them vulnerable.

However, when an opening for a job with the Israeli Foreign Office presented itself, both Lydia and Guydon agreed that they should take a leap of faith and go for it. This was an opportunity too good to miss and the timing felt right. It was time for change. They were full of hope for the future.

And so, they took their first steps out of the desert and entered another kind of world, shaking out the sand from their shoes.

Part 7 New horizons, the curse of the gambler and hope

Morocco

Guydon started off working as a translator for the Israeli Foreign Office but was eventually given the opportunity to work for Mossad (the Institute for Intelligence and Special Operations) as an undercover agent. He was in the right place at the right time to be offered such an opening. And as it turned out, he was the ideal candidate, just the sort of person they were looking for. He had a clean record, was deemed honest, principled and of good character, was fluent in both French and Hebrew, had been a leader in the Youth Movement, possessed all the fine qualities found in a hardworking and disciplined kibbutznik from one of the frontier kibbutzim, thus proving his commitment to the Zionist cause. At that time, Israel held up the kibbutz movement as the pinnacle of its achievements and kibbutzniks were regarded as 'the best of the best'. They had been instrumental in building and inhabiting the Promised Land and were regarded as the cream of the crop. Guydon passed every stage of the recruitment process with flying colours. He gained high scores in all of the tests and examinations. Thorough investigations threw up nothing that might raise concerns. In fact, the unusually high results in his IQ test had impressed the examiner so much that he remarked upon it. Guydon easily met their criteria. This would mark the beginning of a once in a lifetime opportunity which was not to be passed up.

At the time, the Israeli Intelligence Agency was looking to recruit people for Operation Yachin (an operation to secretly emigrate Moroccan Jews to Israel, conducted by Israel's Mossad). Between November 1961 and the spring of 1964 about 97,000 Moroccan Jews left for Israel by plane or ship from Casablanca and Tangier via France and Italy.

> Moroccan Jewish communities constituted the largest of the Jewish communities in North Africa after the Second World War. With the establishment of the state of Israel in 1948, pogroms in Oudja and Jerada together with the fear that eventual independence from France would lead to the persecution of the country's Jews, a large-scale emigration took place. Between 1948 and 1951, 28,000 Moroccan Jews emigrated to Israel. The initial enthusiasm dampened as Moroccan Jews who had emigrated complained of the discrimination they experienced from Ashkenazi Jews in Israel.
>
> After the declaration of Morocco as an independent state in 1956, Jews were granted Moroccan citizenship but with fewer freedoms than the dominant Muslim population, including restrictions on travelling abroad. In 1959, emigration from Morocco to Israel was prohibited (partly due to pressure from the Arab League). Formal prohibition ended in February 1961. However, under the reign of Mohammed V, there was a clear public preference that the Jewish community remain within Morocco and foreign action to facilitate or encourage emigration was barred. Therefore, immigration for the most-part, took place illegally by means of underground Jewish organisations in Morocco, via Spain and France. Mossad made a deal with King Hassan II to clandestinely transport Moroccan Jews to Israel in Operation Yachin, between 1961 and 1964. The peak of Moroccan immigration to Israel took place during those three years. By 1967, 250,000 Jews had left Morocco.

Once Guydon's training was complete, the family were relocated to Paris (early 1960's), from where Guydon travelled to and from Morocco under a false name and passport, posing as a French antique dealer.

Codes had to be used when making contact with other undercover agents in order to confuse the enemy! Clandestine meetings took place, where Guydon wore a jellaba to disguise his face and identity. He appeared as a 'romantic' figure in the eyes of the youth groups he addressed. During these gatherings, it was Guydon's task to encourage and, ultimately, persuade Moroccan Jews to emigrate to Israel. He may have been responsible for government funds which, amongst other things, would have been used to pay for false documents and safe passage to Israel via different routes. He was just one cog within a big wheel of undercover operations at the time.

The work of an undercover agent could be difficult, risky and dangerous. It was important to keep a low profile in order not to arouse suspicion. A solitary existence suited Guydon well and he found playing the role of a French antique dealer exciting.

Guydon was based in Casablanca, a city which amalgamated aspects of French colonial legacy with traditional Arab culture, creating a vibrant and unique atmosphere which he very much enjoyed. He made the most of his time there: learning about antiques, frequenting French restaurants, drinking coffee in Arab cafes, exploring the Souks, visiting the Casino (which he was strictly forbidden to do) and strolling down to the port to watch the Atlantic Ocean roll in. He lived like a carefree bachelor, filling his days with pleasurable pursuits when he was not 'on the job'. He was unencumbered by the demands of everyday family life, far away in both geographical and personal/ emotional ways. He felt free. It was as if he were living two separate lives.

I believe that Guydon experienced his time in Morocco as an adventure and I am far from convinced that he ever truly believed in 'the mission' as such. He was a free thinker and a free spirit first and foremost, never a patriot. He was also reckless and irresponsible at that time.

This was a high point in his life which was to last about three years. And he made the most of it. It could have been the start of a wonderful career. But he blew it. And this is where things became murky and memory so often failed him.

Looking back on this time, he recognised that he had acted selfishly and made grave mistakes and errors of judgement whilst he was there. He admitted (in retrospect) that he had not always acted responsibly during his time in Morocco, as a married man with a family should. And he would pay very dearly for it.

Guydon had his own apartment in Casablanca and the use of a hired car, which gave him independence and the opportunity to explore the country during periods of free time. He visited Fez, Marrakesh, Rabat, Agadir, reaching the foothills of the Atlas Mountains.

Beyond the city walls and gates, he drove out into the countryside and came upon small Berber villages in the hills, where excited children ran down to greet him and Berber women smiled, wearing traditional dresses and jewellery. He watched performances of traditional horsemanship known as 'Tbourida': an ancient Moroccan equestrian art dating back to the 15th century. Riders on horseback charge at the same speed in a line, side by side, whilst firing old muskets into the sky. Also known as 'Fantasia', the spectacle symbolises the strong relationship between man and horse.

He meandered through the old Medina, a labyrinth of interconnecting and winding narrow streets where traders, craftsmen and shopkeepers sold all sorts of wares including, Berber carpets, intricately worked lamps and lanterns, copper teapots and trays, leather goods, textiles, aromatic spices and hanging yarns of brightly coloured wool. In Marrakesh, there were antique shops and antiquarian bookstores to explore. Behind a backdrop of mosques, minarets and magnificent palaces and within the fortifications of Marrakesh was the main square of Jemaa el- Fnaa, a hive of activity and noise with snake charmers, musicians, acrobats, magicians, story-tellers, mystics and gamblers.

The red city of Marrakesh has stood for almost a thousand years: a melting pot of African, European and Arabic influences.

The walls and houses of this medieval city (dating back to the Berber Empire) are made from the red earth and mud found in the surrounding hills, giving this semi- desert city a unique quality. The hot African sun beats down, impregnating the very fabric of the city with a rosy hue. A warm blend of soft peach, terracotta and pink salmon radiate outwards, even under the cover of night.

During his time in Morocco, Guydon acquired a collection of antique Berber jewellery. He bought art books from an elderly Arab bookseller in Casablanca whom he befriended and drank coffee with in his shop, spending many hours there. He bought amethyst stones and crystals by the roadside. But possibly, the most prized purchase of all had been an astrolabe.

Paris

After Guydon's promotion, the family were relocated to Paris where they moved to an apartment in the 16th arrondissement (the most luxurious district in Paris). Apparently, Brigitte Bardot lived in the same street! Eldar (now aged 4 or 5) attended the private Israeli government school. A minibus would collect her in the mornings. Everything was paid for by the Israeli government.

Guydon was away for weeks at a time in Morocco. There was always great excitement on the day of his return. He came laden with marvellous and exotic presents. Eldar could hardly contain herself. It was like Christmas every time he came back! He lavished gifts upon her to try and soften the blow of his long absences.

In many respects, Lydia was wholly unprepared for this new way of life. She had, after all, spent almost a decade in a kibbutz as part of a collective. She felt isolated and lonely in Paris to begin with, as did Eldar. Both their lives seemed to have been turned upside down. Those idyllic, pleasure- filled afternoons Eldar had spent with her father in the kibbutz (where all of her demands could be satisfied) seemed to have vanished overnight.

Daily life was very much confined to indoor living in Paris. It was often overcast, cold and drizzly outside. Le Bois de Boulogne became a favourite haunt, although the weather could never be relied upon. Eldar had to adapt to a new country and climate, a new home and family set- up, a new school, new customs, routines and a new language. In essence, a completely different way of life. Eventually, there would also be a baby sister on the way.

Everything appeared to be going well. What more could a young family wish for starting new beginnings? How fortunate they were! Guydon had good and solid career prospects ahead of him. They were living in the most enviable part of the city. They had received an initial allowance from the Israeli Foreign Office to help them settle in; the future looked bright and promising.

A year before my arrival, there was an outing to 'Theatre des Champs- Elysees' to see the ballet 'Cendrillon' (Cinderella). I have a copy of the original programme (dated 1963- 1964), which is like a piece of artwork in its own right. I had been utterly captivated as a child by the beautiful illustrations of costumes and set designs together with the stylish advertisements for French perfumes.

What was there not to love about Paris with its boutiques and chic department stores, elegant boulevards and avenues, cafes and parks, architecture, romantic bridges, gleaming river, statues and monuments, museums, concert halls, theatres and galleries? It was a beautiful, glittering city. But Lydia felt out of her depth to begin with. She had, after all, been living in a desert for the past ten years!

She had dreaded her first appointment at the hairdresser's, fearing that the stylists would stare at her with sideways glances and judge her. After all, Paris was the centre for 'haute couture' and fashion! She was so out of touch with it all! What would they think of her thick and unruly hair which had been swept by desert winds and left to dry under the hot sun for so long? They would wonder where on earth she had been! In the wilderness!

At the time, the fashion was for the sharp silhouettes of 'Courreges' dresses with hairstyles to match! Chic, modern and sleek! What on earth would they make of her and where would they start?

And although she had desired a more 'conventional' family arrangement, the challenges before her were considerable. All was not ideal or rosy. She had no experience of looking after a young child on her own for such long days. She struggled with ordinary domestic tasks. Shopping for groceries became an ordeal! What should she buy and what should she cook? The choice in the supermarket was overwhelming! Now that she had the chance to choose clothes for her child, she didn't know where to start. She bought Eldar her first raincoat, not having a clue how much she should spend! Of course, she spent far too much and felt woefully inadequate to the task!

She had never dealt with money before. And although Guydon was not on a lavish salary, they had money for the first time in their lives! She had to learn to manage the household finances, to budget and pay bills. This did not come naturally to her as she had no previous experience. Many things had to be learned!

One of the main driving forces underlying the decision to leave the kibbutz was to be able to bring up her children in a 'normal' family setting. She felt that her first child had been born for the collective and, in a way, had been handed over. She did not want to repeat the experience. She wanted exclusive rights over her next child. She had longed to be free to make her own decisions about her children (together with Guydon) and become a proper, autonomously functioning family. What she had not expected or even imagined was the profound sense of loneliness she experienced.

However, Lydia stuck with it, never neglecting her responsibilities or duties. With the passing of time, things improved and gradually became a little easier as she learned how to manage better. She felt less isolated and her confidence grew. Eventually, she befriended another Israeli family with a young child, who were also attached to the Foreign Office and lived in the same apartment block.

Guydon's employment and regular salary enabled my parents to put a deposit down for a flat in a newly constructed block located in one of the emerging suburbs of Tel Aviv. They intended to return there after the three- year posting in Paris, with some money saved up. They started acquiring things to take back with them. There was a solid plan for the future.

Another child was on its way. There was much to look forward to and hope for. They seemed to be shaping a secure future for themselves.

My entry into this world would be very different from Eldar's. Everything was prepared for in advance. My mother wore fetching maternity outfits and purchased the latest and most fashionable baby items from Parisian department stores. There was a beautiful cot and pram, soft blankets and pretty sheets, bottles and formula milk, tiny baby grows and knitted cardigans, booties with satin ribbons, baby creams and lotions. Lydia was able to fulfil all of her fantasies and yearnings. Eldar must have witnessed these items being delivered to the apartment, thinking that the new arrival was already a little princess! Lydia was under the care of a private consultant. Her private hospital room, with its own balcony, was already reserved in La Clinique de la Muette.

On the evening of my arrival, Lydia was making blintzes for the family. Her waters broke as she filled the paper- thin pancakes with soft cream cheese, folding them into the shape of plump pillows. There was no time to finish!

Once I arrived, Lydia had to manage caring for two young children, for the most part on her own. All of her expensive purchases for the new baby did not lighten the load or smooth out the difficulties.

This was both a very joyous and testing time. She relished the possibility of having the new baby all to herself. But then again, she was having to juggle so many things single-handed.

Lydia recounted the story of apple compote to me many times. At one point, I was crying inconsolably for hours on end and she was at her wits end to know what to do. Milk, cuddles, gentle rocking and sweet lullabies were of no avail. She put the tip of her finger in the pot of warm apple compote she had prepared and offered me a tiny amount. The effect was instantaneous and I stopped crying immediately. Soon I was contentedly and soundly asleep, giving everyone some much needed respite for a few hours!

The arrival of a second baby certainly seemed to cast an even longer shadow across Eldar's little life and blight it further. She looked on as her mother doted on and nursed her new charge. She felt shut out, dejected and alone. Mother and baby were like 'queens', seeming to inhabit a beautiful fairytale Queendom from which she felt excluded. Perhaps, if she shut her eyes tightly enough, the vision before her would vanish. Alas, no!

Eldar ached for her father's returns from his trips away. And when he did come back, her life seemed to light up once again. Everything fell into place and was as sweet as before! A sense of the all-consuming joy she had experienced during those balmy, dream-like afternoons in Israel (when she had been at the centre of her parents' attention and affection) could be captured once again, albeit fleetingly. He saved her from her unhappiness. His time at home seemed to pass in a flash whilst his absences seemed to last an eternity. She dreaded the day of his departure when her world, once again, seemed to crumble into a place of gloom and loneliness.

A grave transgression

Whatever the transgression was that irrevocably and unequivocally put an end to Guydon's career will never be fully known or understood. I believe that someone he had been working with in Morocco had alerted HQ of suspected misconduct.

I have guessed (over the years) that it most likely had something to do with the embezzlement of government funds. More than this, I cannot say. Guydon was never transparent about what happened.

In fact, getting to the source of anything with him was nigh on impossible. He buried secrets under layers of confusion, using evasive tactics and charm to wheedle his way out of a tight spot. He liked to present himself as a mysterious and enigmatic figure, often to evade plain, unsavoury truths about himself or his past. He wanted to avoid detection in order to perpetuate myths and deceptions. An air of 'mystique' was created to put us off the scent. Typically, facts were obfuscated.

What I have absolute certainty in, though, is that the slightest question or doubt over his trustworthiness would have been enough to seal his fate and end any future prospects.

Shortly after the family's return to Israel from the posting in Paris, Guydon was subjected to intense cross- examination and questioning. Apparently, he passed the polygraph test. However, too many doubts had been cast over his conduct and too many questions remained unanswered. There would be no second chance and the door shut firmly behind him.

This episode would soon be relegated to the nebulous mists of time and life veered off in a completely new direction, once again.

The road to ruin

The job in Morocco had offered Guydon a unique opportunity and could so easily have developed into an interesting and fulfilling career for him. But it would actually turn out to be his downfall. His gambling addiction was born in Casablanca where he first enjoyed the thrill of the casino, the repercussions of which would blight his life for many years after.

It seems to me that up to this point, Lydia and Guydon had been travelling in the same direction and had shared the same values and vision. However, Guydon's sudden and unexpected expulsion from the Foreign Office marked the beginning of the end of an era when they had once shared common goals. Guydon's unruly hobgoblin had escaped to run amok. Gambling would take centre stage from now onwards, corroding their marriage, creating chaos and instability, leaving us at the mercy of the gods.

The astrolabe

What a beautiful and fascinating object an astrolabe is. This kind of calculator can work out several kinds of problems in astronomy. An ancient, astronomical instrument that was a handheld model of the universe.

Historically, it was used by navigators and astronomers to measure the altitude above the horizon of a celestial body, day or night. It could be used to identify stars and planets, to determine local latitude, to survey or triangulate. It is one of the earliest scientific instruments created to observe celestial and seasonal phenomena.

It was used in classical antiquity, the Islamic Golden Age, the European Middle Ages and the Age of Discovery for all of the above purposes.

The astrolabe's importance comes from the early development of astronomy and determining latitude on land or calm seas. It was used as a navigational aid and to reckon time, giving man a greater understanding and insight into the concept of time and the mysteries of the universe. It was an instrument upon which complex calculations could be achieved to measure the unmeasurable and to give man a deeper understanding of what had hitherto been cloaked in mystery and superstition.

The mariner's astrolabe was developed to use on the heaving deck of a ship in rough seas.

Something caused my father to lose his way in this world. In many respects, he was firmly rooted but in other crucial ways, he allowed himself to drift away on strong currents that led him astray. He threw caution to the wind and headed straight towards unchartered waters, feeling mocked by gods he did not even believe in.

He had once owned an astrolabe but, somehow, he could not hold onto it and it was lost at sea or, perhaps, thrown overboard with a careless gesture. Just as he lost his way during a pivotal time in his life, throwing away a golden opportunity. Without the astrolabe he navigated badly, misread the signs and miscalculated.

Something within him (broken and unhealed) drew him to squally seas and chaos. His failure to steer a steady course led him straight into the eye of the storm.

He had the astrolabe in his hands and it could have been used wisely. Instead, it was cast aside, leaving Guydon adrift and at the mercy of tempests and gigantic waves which tossed him about cruelly, this way and that.

Revelations

Much later on, Guydon revealed (with a certain air of regret) that he had once owned a beautiful astrolabe which he had acquired in Morocco together with a significant collection of Berber jewellery. I had never seen any of these treasures because he had sold them (desperate for money as always) in a Parisian auction house for a pittance.

It does not seem out of the question that the proceeds from the sale of the above items (which were sold under pressure and in haste) were used to replace government funds which Guydon had been entrusted with to pay for the procurement of false documents and the safe passage of Jewish Moroccans to Israel. What had he done with the embezzled money? Had he needed it to cover mounting gambling and mortgage debts? I will never know the complete truth.

Guydon resorted to vagueness when a simple and direct explanation was called for. I never knew a time when he was not under financial pressure. Getting his life back on track was a constant struggle. He seemed doomed to fail even before he started.

Guydon was only too aware that he had let a rare opportunity slip though his fingers and trickle away like water. He had been unable to keep his impulses under check. The routine and discipline of kibbutz life had provided that essential containment.

Over the course of his life, many things were sold or lost irretrievably.

And so it would continue in the same fashion for some time.

Yafo (Jaffa)

After Guydon's mission in Morocco ended, the family were sent back to Israel and moved into the flat they had purchased in Tel Aviv which was heavily mortgaged. Guydon resumed his work as a translator for a short time (looking at news from all over the world that might be useful to intelligence) whilst awaiting a new assignment 'out in the field'.

However, I believe questions over his conduct, whilst being an undercover agent in Morocco, had already begun. It was not long after his return from Paris that a very thorough investigation began which involved interrogations, searches and lie detectors. He was under suspicion.

Trust had been breached and he was quickly cast out of the Intelligence Bureau. His dismissal was final and absolute.

He kept the complete truth from my mother and she never discovered exactly what had happened. Agents conducted a search of the family home. She was not told what they might be looking for. She guessed it might be money or expensive purchases that could not be accounted for. It was a humiliating and undignified experience for her, with young children at home.

However, the family were not left to the mercy of the wolves and a position of employment was offered to Guydon (taking into account his knowledge and interest in antiques) as the sales manager of an antiques and art gallery in Yafo which belonged to a Frenchman by the name of Jean Tiroche.

Guydon worked in the gallery for about 2- 3 years. Tiroche had been one of the first entrepreneurs to settle in Yafo and open a gallery there. He owned several paintings by the artist, Emmanuel Mane-Katz, who is best known for his depictions of the Jewish shtetl in Eastern Europe. Several of his paintings hung in the gallery. There was also a painting of a cat by the Japanese-French painter, Foujita, priced at 8,000 dollars. Today it would be worth closer to a million!

Guydon learned a great deal about art from Tiroche who was very knowledgeable and had a good eye. However, he had been a bit of a crook in the past and had spent some time in prison for tax evasion.

Tiroche went into partnership with an American millionaire and they expanded the business to include furniture bought from various auction houses all over Europe. Guydon managed the shop during Tiroche's absences and tried to sell the furniture. But the venture was not successful and the gallery did not do well. People simply didn't have that kind of money to spend on luxury items then.

Yafo is an ancient port city located in the southern and oldest part of Tel Aviv, boasting a rich history. The shop was located somewhere amongst the old, narrow passageways and courtyards. Yafo is a melting pot of Jewish and Arab populations, where modernity and antiquity intertwine. Guydon would frequent Arab cafes, enjoying Arabic coffee and Middle Eastern food: freshly baked flat bread with hummus, soft cheeses, eggs, olives, cucumber and tomato or a delicious shakshuka for breakfast. There was a vibrant and lively atmosphere. He zipped around on a scooter, whizzing past ancient, sand coloured stone houses and vaulted archways. Winding, cobbled streets sloped up and down. There was the hint of a warm sea breeze in the air and the glinting turquoise waters of the Mediterranean Sea lapped against the limestone walls of the old harbour.

Guydon was gambling heavily during this period, playing cards with Tiroche and other antique and art dealers. He was in serious arrears with his mortgage payments, debts were mounting and he found himself unable to support the family. There were rumours that he had also played a dishonest hand whilst in charge of the gallery, taking money for his own personal use. Tiroche sacked him.

He was running out of options. There was no question of returning to the kibbutz and, due to the nature of his dismissal from the Foreign Office, most avenues were closed off to him. He found himself in 'a bit of a fix'.

We were penniless and desperate. Our next port of call would be London. But before that, yet another war.

Tomatoes and The Six Day War: 5th-10th June 1967

As a reservist, Guydon was called up by the Israeli army for the Six Day War. He had previously been trained in defusing land mines. He could detect where the mines might be hidden by testing the soil. Then, earth would be gently scraped away around the mine and the detonator unscrewed to render it harmless.

This was a very fast-moving situation. He was then assigned to the Ambulance Corps. His main duty was to bring out the wounded from the front line. He was a stretcher bearer and had received enough basic training in first aid to be able to administer to the wounds of the injured. As a child, I remember that Guydon seemed to possess a good general knowledge in first aid. He dealt with minor domestic ailments or accidents with competence, confidence and calm, always seeming to know what to do and make good decisions. I always felt I was in safe hands.

The army was on the move constantly and he tried to keep as low a profile as possible in order to stay alive! There was no time to eat. At one stop, Guydon filled his billy can, pockets and helmet with tomatoes picked from the fields, which kept him going for three days.

Guydon was in Jerusalem when it was conquered, reaching the Western Wall. He belonged to one of the first units that freed Jerusalem from the Jordanian army. Apparently, they fled quickly and did not put up much resistance. He picked up a policeman's truncheon from a Jordanian Police Station as war booty, which I still have today.

During this brief episode, Lydia was in Tel Aviv with me and Eldar, trying to manage on her own yet again. She remembered that it was a time of great tension, fear and uncertainty. Instead of going down to the shelter with the other residents when the siren rang out, she decided to stay inside the apartment, preferring to bundle us into bed so that we could cuddle up together. She didn't like the man who had put himself in charge of the block during Guydon's absence. She refused to obey his instructions! Edzia had been sending tubes of condensed milk to us, which we sucked on with delight under the bedcovers! I was two years old and Eldar was eight.

After the war, Guydon returned safely. Shortly, the family were to face different and more personal challenges.

The Six Day War, 1967. Guydon is the one smoking!

London: A brief history

When we arrived in London (1968) we moved in with Edzia and Benny (her second husband) who was a successful businessman at the time in the East End rag trade and he owned two hotels in Kings Cross. The four of us shared one room in our grandmother's two-bedroomed flat for two years. Guydon and Lydia worked in the Regina Hotel. The intention was for them to pay off their debts and mortgage arrears so that they could return to Israel with a clean slate and try to make a go of things (my father's dismissal from the Foreign Office and his consequent gambling had left the family in dire financial straits). They worked long hours: making beds, cleaning rooms, taking care of the laundry, making breakfast. They were used to hard physical work but this was a million miles away from their experience in the kibbutz and under very different circumstances. As a child, all I remember about the Regina Hotel was a lingering mustiness mixed with the smell of fried eggs and bacon and the bright orange bedspreads.

Much later on, I learned that whilst managing the hotel, Guydon had been caught pilfering. He was sacked by Benny immediately.

Edzia most probably pleaded with Benny to give her daughter and son-in-law a second chance, if only for the sake of the children!

Benny agreed to help my parents, by putting up the capital for them to run a snack-bar independently, hoping that they would be able to make a go of it and, finally, stand on their own two feet!

They worked like horses, buying the produce they needed in the early hours of the morning before opening up the snack-bar to prepare breakfast and serve customers. But it didn't work out. This was not the life they wanted for themselves and the business quickly folded.

Lydia would say that this was the worst time of her life. She could barely bring herself to think about those days. All had been lost. They had nothing. She described how she made herself numb so as not to feel anything. This was the only way she could carry on. She hid all of her feelings from Edzia. Once again, she felt she owed her mother gratitude for 'saving' them. How could she express any feelings of anger, frustration, hurt or despair under the circumstances? She went through the motions of living, whilst feeling empty and dead inside.

At the same time, the lure of London casinos proved too strong a temptation for Guydon to resist and so began a very long, intense and harmful period of gambling. Most of his earnings were frittered away in these seedy establishments. The flat in Israel eventually had to be sold to pay off mortgage arrears and mounting debts.

These were very dark times, although we didn't know or feel any of this as children.

We never returned to Israel and ended up staying in London permanently, becoming naturalized British Citizens. Benny and Edzia had, at one time, offered to support Guydon in studies of his own choosing or on a training programme. He could have used his knowledge of languages in some capacity. But he refused.

Eventually, Benny suggested 'The Knowledge' and Guydon became a London cabbie. Mastering 'The Knowledge' typically takes three to four years as it is very challenging. But I'm pretty sure Guydon managed it in half that time. I remember he had a scooter with a clipboard attached to the front with a long list of street names and famous London landmarks. He would set off early in the morning, whizzing around London until the complex map of this vast, sprawling and wonderful city was firmly imprinted on his mind. I think he enjoyed this experience. Once again, he had a sense of freedom, purpose and excitement. And so, he became part of one of the best taxi services in the world, not least because London cabbies know the quickest routes through London's complicated road network and hold an encyclopaedic knowledge of the city in their memories.

This was a good move. It enabled Guydon to become his own boss, whilst being able to earn a living and support the family. He was master of his own time and movements. He was independent. That suited him. We finally moved out of my grandmother's flat and into our own accommodation: renting the flat above the shops (which I have already described in some detail). He was a London cabbie for many years, still driving in his eighties until he became too ill.

Later on, I discovered that research had been carried out which showed that London cab drivers have uniquely larger hippocampi than almost anyone else. The hippocampus is the part of the brain that controls spacial intelligence. The navigational demands of driving stimulate this area of brain development.

Guydon was a very good driver and knew his way around London confidently, taking small back streets, weaving and winding about. I loved sitting in the back of the cab (rain or shine), taking in the spectacle and atmosphere of this great city with its magnificent Royal Parks and elegant buildings. Tall, majestic London Plane trees, with their distinctive peeling bark (the lungs of this great city), lined the avenues we drove through, casting dappled light and shade on the shiny black bonnet and roof of his taxi, a green canopy above and around us, creating a shimmering, scintillating light during summer months.

However, despite being in full employment as a taxi driver, there were always money problems with Guydon, even after he quit the gambling tables for good.

At some point, he must have recognised how much was at stake and in peril. His marriage was a wreck from which there was no guarantee of salvage. His finances were in a perpetual state of disarray. He was never far away from financial ruin and bankruptcy. He was constantly trying to dig himself out of a very deep hole. Yet somehow, the hole kept filling up again.

Eventually, Lydia went back to college and managed to acquire enough qualifications to complete a degree and become a teacher of French Language and Literature in Higher Education. Quite an achievement, I think. She had always been clever and full of promise. Finally, she was able to earn a living and have her own money for the first time in her life. Independence, at last!

Eldar had to adapt, once again, to a new country, culture and language.

Initially, I think we both struggled to settle. However, later on, as adults, we managed to find a niche for ourselves and call London our home.

The marriage, however, had been put under enormous strain, leaving it in tatters. The gambling had done its worst.

A complex character

As a London cabbie, Guydon enjoyed a certain amount of freedom and independence, which suited his nature and personality. He was never one to stay on a well-trodden path. He was always tempted to stray off and veer away from the beaten track. Getting lost was far more interesting than knowing where you were going. The prospect of an adventure was more appealing and tantalising than the humdrum of ordinary, everyday life. Distractions were irresistible. These characteristics (amongst others) made Guydon interesting and different.

However, years of gambling had created multiple layers of unfathomable complication in Guydon's life: a tangled web which led to many a dead end.

But this is only part of the story. Guydon was a dedicated and patient father. He loved his children unconditionally and we were never far away from his thoughts. He only ever had our best interests at heart. He supported us and always did what he could for us. He was not an absent or remote figure. On the contrary, he was (for the most part) reachable and available. He often brought out the best in people.

Not only did my parents share the same 'beginnings', philosophy and political outlook on life but also a common devotion to their children. On this matter, they were united and trod the same path. They held out a beacon for both of us, lighting our way. On other matters, they walked alone and the road forked off in opposite directions.

I have previously described Guydon as a traveller on the Silk Road. He loved the London antique markets, particularly Portobello. Always on the lookout for treasure, he brought many fascinating and attractive objects home to us. He enjoyed detective work and liked nothing more than delving into his collection of reference books to uncover clues that might help him solve mysteries surrounding certain objects. He often did this with us, teaching us to be curious and inquiring and to keep our sense of wonder alive. He indulged us, purchasing little trinkets from the markets and encouraged collecting. For example, he built up a collection of Russian Dolls and ethnic jewellery for me.

He helped me with my school work, especially maths and essay writing! His command of the English language was fantastic. Guydon described his first lesson in English to me (so many years ago in Belgium) when he had been taught and never forgot the phrase: '*My tailor is rich*'. I always felt we learned together (as equals) peering into dictionaries and encyclopaedias for definitions and information. He made me understand the joy of learning and encouraged intellectual curiosity. Life was an enchantment with Guydon. He could turn everything, even the most mundane, into an adventure or a moment of magic. He possessed a unique talent for this. I remember dangling cherries on my ears like jewellery and cutting out mouths with funny teeth from orange peel. He had a special whistle (from the Youth Movement days), a little tune to call his tribe when we got lost in the woods searching for acorns and conkers! What good company and fun he was! I never felt lonely with him. He was generous with his time. He was playful, open- minded and affectionate. We played Scrabble and Monopoly, card games and he taught us chess. He was genuinely interested in us as people. He made it his business to be there for us, through thick and thin, no matter what. We adored him!

I remember the day 'The Encyclopaedia Britannica' arrived. This was a very exciting moment, which we had been anticipating for some time. Guydon was paying for it by monthly instalments. Education was important as was an appreciation for art. I remember him taking down art books from the shelf and introducing me to French impressionists like Renoir, Monet, Cezanne. He showed me breathtakingly beautiful winter landscapes by Pieter Bruegel the Elder. Guydon shared his love of art, in all its forms. I remember helping him polish small items of silver which he had purchased from the markets. Pierre-Auguste Renoir was one of his favourite artists. He had expressed deep tenderness for the painting, 'Dance at Bougival'. He referred to Picasso as a titan.

On his way home from driving the cab in central London, he would often stop off at a Jewish bakery in Golder's Green to buy

Bourekas (pastries) filled with feta cheese, mashed potato and spinach, Baba ganoush (aubergine dip), chopped liver, Challah, cheesecake, chocolate Babka, honey or poppyseed cake and sweet Lokshen Kugel. These foods connected both him and Lydia to their roots and childhood.

Over the years, he had collected glass paperweights. The most sought- after ones were French, made in the classic years between 1845-1860. There were three important factories at the time: Clichy, Saint Louis and Baccarat. Each produced weights in their own particular style featuring unique motifs. For example, Clichy is famous for its Clichy rose and beautiful bouquet arrangements, Baccarat made complex millefiori (thousand flowers) weights and Saint Louis produced paperweights featuring fruits and vegetables. All three factories produced exquisite lampwork paperweights which incorporated stylised flowers, butterflies, snakes and lizards embedded inside the glass domes. Initials and dates might be hidden within the close packed millefiori, under a leaf or between the petals of a flower. You had to look closely.

It was virtually impossible to come across one of these prized and increasingly rare objects whilst scouring the markets in the early hours of the morning, scanning items in semi- darkness with a torch. Guydon's collection was eclectic. He did not possess highly valuable examples. Nevertheless, he took pleasure from and was able to appreciate each one, even those that were damaged, chipped or cracked. He never rejected imperfect or broken things. His vision was wide and inclusive, in both literal and metaphorical terms. He found beauty and interest in many things and in many ways. The notion of 'perfection' did not carry greater worth in his mind. He valued all sorts of things. And I do wonder whether this assortment of broken bits and pieces he had collected over the years might not hold another meaning altogether. The loss of his brothers, Simon and Abraham, had left the family broken and incomplete. Guydon, I always believed, also had a broken part within him (deep and hidden).

Guydon never gave up hope or lost interest in the world, despite doing battle with some pretty tenacious demons over his lifetime. A steady flame burned inside him, reflecting his many unique qualities and charms, even during the darkest of days. Deadlocks did not prevent him from experiencing life as a voyage of discovery. And yet, he had a blind spot, which could lead to wastelands of desolation and wretchedness.

It would seem contradictory to describe him as both an optimist and a fatalist. But that is what he was, with lots of shades in between. He is not an easy person to describe or understand. Encapsulating him is rather impossible. He escapes being pinned down. He remains largely elusive and mysterious, just as he wanted. It is all part of the plan.

He seemed to be the sum part of many opposites. You felt completely safe and protected by him, but you also felt that you were left vulnerable. He made himself available to you, but he was also maddeningly evasive. He brought you hope and yet you sensed a tragic element within him. He wanted the best for you, but could not find it for himself. He made things possible and impossible at the same time. He was warm, generous and open but also difficult to reach. The world in his eyes was limitless but also full of dead ends. He 'lit up' a room whilst at the same time dimming the switch to a low, shadowy light. He brought optimism and cheer as well as a more bleak and dismal vision. He lived in a world of contradictions that made perfect sense to him, but not so much to others. He was complicated and unfathomable. He escapes definition. What a conundrum!

What is the landscape, the sum total of a person's life? It is not one thing but many. And in Guydon's case, it was layer upon layer of complexities and dichotomies. He eludes fitting into neat and satisfying descriptions or narratives.

He was certainly courageous, adventurous and imaginative. He had a genuine warmth which people connected with immediately.

He possessed a capacity for abstract, creative and original thought and observed the 'surreal' in everyday life. He had resilience to combat despair, tragedy and the darker places we inhabit. He was nostalgic and secretly sentimental. He often thought of the comfort of others before his own. He could be accused of many wrong- doings and misdemeanours; a serious lack of judgement at times. Yes, he had been foolish. Yet he was also wise and insightful. He could be enigmatic and cryptic. He did not achieve what so many thought he would achieve with his sharpness of mind, intelligence and personal qualities. That 'touch of brilliance' (which everyone had recognised in him as a child) had come into conflict with a destructive force which extinguished possibilities. So much wasted potential, they would say! He could get distracted easily. He had allowed himself to enter forbidden places which would, ultimately, cause harm to both himself and others.

Homage to a great city

After moving in with Edzia and Benny for two years, my parents finally ended up staying in London permanently and making an independent life for themselves here.

My personal attachment to this wonderful city is very much connected to the notion that my parents were able to find a sense of belonging and place here.

I had often thought about a hundred 'What ifs?' to myself over the years, knowing that there had been many twists and turns in my parents' story. I had witnessed painful struggles between them. They appeared to be keeping a semblance of a marriage together for the children's sake. The seams of this marriage were frayed and falling apart, the stitching undone and seemingly beyond repair. In so many ways, they brought misery to one another and were not well suited. But they never separated, despite having discussed the possibility a thousand times over, whilst burning the midnight oil.

London gave Guydon a means of earning a living (without compromising his sense of freedom) and the thrill of the antique markets. Finally, Lydia was able to gain a sense of independence and grow into a woman, carving out a professional life for herself.

London has made room for all of us.

Coffee and Bourbons

I try to imagine a typical morning in London when Guydon was a taxi driver. He wakes up very early in order to get to the markets before starting his working day. We are all soundly asleep in our warm beds and cosy duvets, still dreaming. I imagine he relishes this quiet time which he can call his own. He prepares a strong cup of instant black coffee with a little sugar to sweeten the bitterness. He dunks in a couple of Bourbons. This is his pre-breakfast repast. He lights a cigarette in the cab before switching on the engine and making his way to Portobello. The end of his cigarette burns like an ember in the early morning gloom. The streets are empty, the roads are quiet. Light is beginning to filter through the dark, early morning, pushing the day forward. Perhaps he listens to the voice of Miriam Makeba (a South African singer/ songwriter he enjoyed) on the tape as he drives through London at dawn.

This is much like his early starts in kibbutz Gvulot, all those years ago. He made coffee on the little stove in their room. He took out a little biscuit or sweet cake from the old tin. Darkness was falling off the shoulders of the emerging day. Soon streaks of orange and purple would break through before the eruption of searing heat and dazzling light. But first this quiet before the day stirred itself into motion. Just enough time to water the cactus and amaryllis plants growing in pots on the veranda. Just enough time to fill pans with fresh, cool water for the little visiting birds which appeared like sprites out of air. He jumped into the jeep and made his way to the open fields. The air was still and cool, as he wound down the window. The light quickened and changed fast. Soon the onslaught of midday sun and blistering heat. He experienced a sense of freedom and purpose. He was master of his own destiny as he drove into the desert, leaving a trail of dust behind him. This was his time and his moment, like no other before or since. Life had a predictable and pleasant rhythm which suited him well during those early years.

A superstitious atheist and the end of the Silk Road

The deeper gamblers fall into the pit of their addiction, the more obscure and opaque their accounts become. Part of their life gets tangled up like a tight knot that cannot be unpicked. So many things become unnecessarily and unfathomably complicated in order to disguise simple truths. A web of deceits and falsehoods (spun over the most intense period of gambling) eventually entraps them. Along the way, much is irretrievably lost and damaged: prospects, opportunity, a marriage, financial security and the chance for any kind of normal existence is considerably diminished.

I will always have an image of the piles of unopened correspondence in brown envelopes sitting on the sideboard at home. Unpaid bills, tax demands, loans. A trail of financial mess seemed to follow Guydon everywhere.

But I also like to think of him as a traveller along the Silk Road. And although the reality of his life had turned out limited and prosaic for one with such shining potential, he had the capacity to travel anywhere within his mind. He opened up our imaginations. He only ever wanted to give us good things and a sense of hope and possibility. Although he himself sometimes dwelt in a darker place, he wanted to make us believe in a world that was bright and intriguing, full of beguiling and wondrous things. He kept our dreams illuminated and alive.

I recall an old gramophone that he once owned on which he played old, crackling records, voices and music from a long time ago. Sometimes he listened to classical music (I distinctly remember 'The Four Seasons' by Vivaldi), Jazz Sebastian Bach Les Swingle Singers and songs by Jacques Brel. He did not seem to have much time for these little pleasures, though.

I think, towards the end of his life, there was nowhere for him to hide or run to. He had reached the end of the Silk Road. He knew it. His life had been what it was and there was no time left to make reparation to those whom he had let down and hurt the most, namely my mother. This is how he saw things and they pressed on him heavily, like iron weights.

He believed that he had been dogged by bad fortune and that 'luck' had eluded him. He described 'luck' and 'bad luck' as if they were real and malevolent beings who had thwarted him all of his life, running rings around him and snapping at his heels like a pack of rabid dogs frothing at the mouth. He once wrote, '*I will have to catch this devil by the tail*'. He believed that his life had been plagued by little demons.

What he failed to see was that it had all been of his own making. It came from within and could have been quietened down, tamed and gained control of, if only he had taken ownership of it to be able to discover its origin and source.

A deeper explanation

Guydon had referred to the Moroccan period as 'the wilderness years', meaning a period of abandon and recklessness. He did not consider the Negev as a place of wilderness because the kibbutz environment had offered a containing, purposeful and disciplined way of life which brought out the best in him and kept him on the 'straight and narrow'.

Morocco (the promise of opportunity and new horizons) was, in reality, the beginning of his downfall.

I wonder whether experiences in his early life had played some role in the chaos that was to become part of his make- up and shape much of his future life.

As we already know, Moishe and Mariem had not allowed the name of their two eldest sons (Simon and Abraham) ever to be mentioned again after the war. If the memory of what had passed was buried, then perhaps it could be forgotten and vanish, making life possible.

When Guydon returned home to his parents after the war had ended (at the age of 12 years), he had expected to be re-united with his older brothers too. But instead, he discovered that they were mysteriously absent. Not only that, but there was an impenetrable silence surrounding this fact. It was forbidden to speak of them. He was told nothing. Something so unimaginably terrible was being kept from him as to render it unmentionable. It must be erased. It must be made to disappear entirely. Perhaps that feeling never really left Guydon and he carried it inside him all his life. Deeply buried, just like the names of Simon and Abraham, whose faces would slowly fade from the minds of those who had loved them, turning into half-remembered fragments and scraps.

Had Guydon's more destructive side somehow emerged from that tragic event? The brutal murder of two brothers in the gas chambers of Auschwitz. The terrible shame and guilt that cast a shadow over the family. A sense of something terrifyingly dark, intangible and unfathomable.

It was never spoken of. Yet, it was there all the time.

Did the faces of their two lost sons only appear to Moishe and Mariem in their dreams, like watery spirits mingling with the swaying seagrasses at the bottom of the seabed or in the smog of a poisonous, yellow gas?

Can it be said of Guydon that he had acted on destructive impulses because the tragedy of what had happened to his two elder brothers and family was never spoken about and never brought into the light? It was unspeakable. The truth was smothered, leaving no opportunity for anyone to come to terms with that terrible event. The tragedy that had befallen the family was suppressed and hidden, as if everyone's life depended on it. The memory was stifled, denied oxygen and words. Two names fading and burning out at the same time. No healing was possible. The memory was cut out like a festering sore. However, the truth is that Simon and Abraham have always had their rightful place in the story. And through the telling of it, we can finally begin to let go and understand. The world does not end. In fact, it goes on and becomes brighter.

Cherry blossom and the Minotaur's lair

After Guydon's death (12th April 2017) I noticed the pink and white blossom on the tree outside the window of his and Lydia's flat in London. He had always appreciated the blossom on this tree, which left a soft, velvety skirt of petals underneath it.

Lydia had selected a simple arrangement of green foliage for Guydon's funeral. A bouquet of bear grass, aspidistra and eucalyptus leaves tied with natural twine was placed on top of the coffin.

It was devastating to lose him and although expected, it was a shock nonetheless. We suffered without him. His absence did not seem real for a very long time.

The sight of the coffin was ghastly. It was unimaginable to believe that he was gone. He had always roamed so freely and occupied such a strong and defined place within the landscape of our imaginations and minds.

Guydon had been like a magician. He tried to cover his tracks with 'sleight of hand'. He was a player, a conjuror of tricks and illusionist. Master of the intangible, the slippery, the disappearing.

I am reminded of Mr. Mistoffelees from T.S. Eliot's 'Old Possum's Book of Practical Cats':

> *You ought to know Mr. Mistoffelees!*
> *The Original Conjuring Cat-*
> *(There can be no doubt about that).*
> *Please listen to me and don't scoff. All his*
> *Inventions are off his own bat.*
> *There's no such Cat in the metropolis;*
> *He holds all the patent monopolies*
> *For performing surprising illusions*
> *And creating eccentric confusions.*
> *At prestidigitation*
> *And at legerdemain*
> *He'll defy examination*
> *And deceive you again.*
> *The greatest magicians have something to learn*
> *From Mr. Mistoffelees' Conjuring Turn.*
> *Presto!*
> *Away we go!*
> *And we all say: OH!*
> *Well I never!*
> *Was there ever*
> *A Cat so clever*
> *As Magical Mr. Mistoffelees!*

(Verse 1 from Mr. Mistoffelees by T.S. Eliot)

Gamblers are innately superstitious, even if they happen to be atheists. They believe that they are at the mercy of 'Lady Luck' on every spin of the roulette wheel. It can go either way for them. But ultimately, it is out of their hands. There is a greater force at large and in operation.

Not long after Guydon took his first steps out of Kibbutz Gvulot, things started to unravel ruinously. Little demons were let loose, to wreak havoc and do their worst. They laughed and pranced about as they went on the rampage. They deceived and duped. They have no conscience. They feel no remorse or pity. They play with you like a 'thing', a puppet on a string.

Guydon felt that he had been entrapped and tricked by these invisible imps and pranksters, the jokers in the pack. But they were of his own making and conjuring and could have been dispelled with one breath.

Instead, he allowed them to toy with him and lead him down dark and labyrinthine passageways where he would encounter the Minotaur. But rather than face the creature, he ran from it, using all the tricks up his sleeve.

To take ownership of one's darker side diminishes its power and influence. If we allow the rogue monster to surface from the hidden depths (the centre of the maze) it will be revealed to us so that we may understand and fear it less. Then we can look it straight in the eye, acknowledge it politely (doffing our caps), cut it down to size, put it in its place, resist its allure, part from it amicably and feel at liberty to go our separate ways.

Otherwise, the little fiend will always have a claim over us. We will never be entirely free to choose our own destiny and shape our own life.

As the years passed, this restless little spirit that had dwelt somewhere within Guydon was finally tamed and quietened down, mellowing with age until it disappeared altogether...

I can conjure up Guydon whenever I like. I always have access to him although he is no longer here. The dialogue between us continues, just as the delicate blossom falls each year upon the grass. His disappearing act is not all that it seems!

The banana incident

There was one incident when Guydon was in hospital (very ill with terminal cancer), which illustrates his quirky way of thinking about things; his humour, playfulness and connection with the surreal and absurd in everyday life (which never left him) and always entertained us. Lydia asked: *"Well, what did the consultant say this morning?"* Guydon looked at us with that warm twinkle in his eye (a spark of mischief) and gesturing towards the banana on his tray he replied, *"Ask the banana..."* So absurd and yet it made us laugh and broke the tension during such a difficult time. This was how he often eluded a straightforward response and also how he dealt with adversity. Humour was his greatest defence.

The nearness of death can bring intimacy and greater understanding

Only at the end of his life (facing a diagnosis of terminal cancer and very limited time) was the truth (in all its nakedness) laid bare before Guydon. He still possessed charm and typical good humour. But with Lydia, there was a reckoning. The truth tormented him. He recognised and admitted, for the first time during those last months of his life, that he had plunged Lydia (and therefore the family also) into a life of chaos and gloom which was of his own making. The life he had made for himself had left Lydia vulnerable, without security, money or any kind of future. He regretted it deeply. Rather than be with her, he had chosen to escape into a dark and secret world of his own. He couldn't explain why he had behaved like this. He could only reassure her that he had always loved her and had wanted to be with her. None of it had been her fault.

He apologised repeatedly, as if he could not process the enormity of what had been. He confessed to his flaws and weaknesses repeatedly, as if he were revealing them for the first time, believing that he had been successful in hiding them so perfectly when, in reality, nothing could have been further from the truth. The 'shadows' that had been cast upon the family landscape were in plain sight, if you chose to look and see. There was something quite sad and pitiful about it all.

Lydia finally understood that he had never wanted to abandon her. His destructive behaviour was something inexplicable to him. He regretted all of his foolishness which had led to a catalogue of unfortunate events. He felt that he had failed her and despair turned to remorse.

Finally, it could all be laid to rest and they were able to find some peace together during the last months of Guydon's life where forgiveness, tenderness, understanding and reconciliation could replace years of conflict, resentment, recrimination and bitter disappointment.

At last, I think they understood how vulnerable they had both been, coming from the same place after all. That unbreakable bond which had held them together through quite a tortured marriage, turned out to be as complex, intricate and strong as the delicately woven threads of a spider's web.

April

Both of my beautiful parents, Lydia and Guydon, died during the month of April at the age of 83, only three years apart. The final curtain at the end of a long and eventful life together.

The pathways to the crematorium meander through fields of headstones which seem to hem you in, making you feel apprehensive and somewhat suffocated. It is a long and circuitous route as you follow the signs. Finally, after what seems like an endless drive, a clearing up ahead. There stands the crematorium, a sombre looking building with a glass dome and large oak doors. One might describe the architecture as simple, understated and quietly dignified.

Your eyes cannot avert the raised coffin at the back of the black hearse. But it is too frightful! Then you notice that the tall trees and flower garden surrounding the crematorium are reflected upon the shiny glass windows of the hearse like a picture. It is a warm spring day. The sun's rays caress you momentarily as you stroll through the garden of remembrance, delaying the moment you have to go into the building. The pallbearers lift the coffin out of the hearse and carry it into the crematorium. They wear frockcoats, top hats and gloves. For a moment it looks like a scene from a novel by Dickens. The funeral director shakes my hand limply but his hushed words of condolence are lost on me.

Inside, the coffin has already been placed on its plinth, centre front. There are neat rows of seats with comfortable, square shaped teal cushions. A quiet light floods the space and there is an air of peace. Music plays and there are some images to watch on a large screen that flicker past.

Finally, a green velvet curtain closes silently in front of you and the coffin disappears behind it whilst you utter your final goodbye. Somewhere, cherry blossom falls without a sound, forming a carpet of delicate pink and white petals upon the ground, as if tipped out from the upturned hat of a magician.

Parallel lives and suitcases

As children during the war years, it was as if my parents had lived parallel lives. Both of their families had come from Eastern Europe which would witness the systematic murder of the Jewish people and the bloodbath of the Nazi extermination camps. Both sets of families had emigrated to Belgium and had then tried to flee from the Nazi hordes in 1940. Both Lydia and Guydon had been placed in hiding with new identities. The first experience had been unpleasant for both of them, the second was more positive (particularly for Lydia). They were caught up in a living nightmare, separated from their parents (who needed to go into hiding themselves in order to survive) not knowing what the future would hold. They both lived out the remainder of the war in the Ardennes, in a landscape featuring castles and forests straight out of a children's fairy tale. And then there was Hashomer Hatzair, which was the beginning of their love story and a lifelong union.

After we moved into our North London flat above the shops, a large, black steamer trunk with shiny brass locks arrived. It had all sorts of intriguing labels stuck over it, having travelled from Paris to Israel and finally to London. Inside the trunk, were some of my parents' precious possessions. The oriental cloisonné candlesticks, letters and photographs, dried pressed desert flowers tumbling out of the pages of *Voyages Extraordinaires* by Jules Vernes, an assortment of art books, French novels, a large amethyst crystal, butterscotch amber beads, Daum glassware, hand beaten copper jars from Morocco and a giant black teddy bear!

How many suitcases have featured in this story? How much packing, travelling and unpacking? And finally, a large, brass bound cabin trunk lands on our doorstep in London, the final stop.

Edwarda's story described immense journeys with valises and vanity cases containing secret compartments. She had traversed vast distances and lived through huge political upheaval and social turmoil. The Russian Revolution, the Great Depression and two world wars!

When Lydia was in hospital for the last time, I quickly packed a small overnight bag for her with some toiletries and a clean change of clothes. Deep down, I knew these items would not be needed.

At the end (on the last part of our journey) we have no use for belongings. We leave this world empty handed. It is all left behind us. The Chagall book tucked away in a drawer, her last written notes lying on the dining room table, the silver candlesticks on the mantlepiece, the precious wine glasses from Russia, her letters to Guydon and his to her, thoughts and words vanishing into an emptying space.

Final thoughts

There is an old Victorian churchyard near my house. Some of the inscriptions on the headstones in the garden of remembrance have faded and disappeared over time. The grass has been left to grow tall and wild. This place is a haven for wildlife. Once I saw a fox. It was a fleeting encounter. He stopped dead in his tracks (as still as a statue) and stared at me for a very brief moment, before vanishing into the undergrowth as silently as he had appeared. The yew trees are very old too, left to grow naturally. Birdsong can be heard. But apart from that, it is a very quiet and still place. There is never anyone here. An area which is kept tidy has more recent graves; I often find freshly laid flowers there. I like to read the names, dates and inscriptions: final words of remembrance and love. Many graves have not been visited for a very long time; there is an air of neglect and abandonment about them. Perhaps too much time has passed and there is nobody who remembers anymore.

A rare strawberry moon hovering in the blue- indigo night sky, reminds us that life is small, transient and fragile, but also expansive, far- reaching and encompassing. It always has its beginning and its end.

As I stroll through the churchyard, reading all of the words carefully chiselled in stone, I have a sense of love surviving and continuing. It can be felt in the gentle breeze, in the stirring and restlessness of the long, wild grass and in the warmth of the sun on a late summer's afternoon.

I requested 'La Mer' by Charles Tenet to be played at Lydia's funeral service. It reminded me of her childhood seaside holidays by the Belgian coast; of dreams, hopes and joys at the very beginning of life.

Post-kibbutz years in Israel, Morocco and Paris

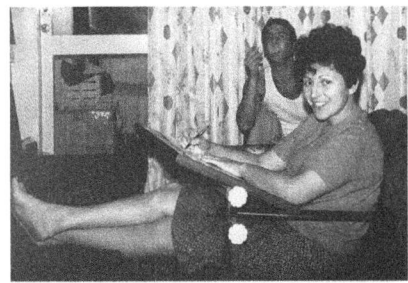

Guydon and Lydia planning their next move from Israel

Lydia with baby Lena born in 1965, Paris

Guydon at the foothills of the Atlas Mountains, Morocco 1960's

Lydia and Guydon in Paris, 1960's

London Years: from the late 1960's onwards

Lydia and Guydon outside the Regina Hotel

Guydon becomes a London cabbie!

Beautiful Lydia!

Treasure trove!

APPENDIX 1
Chana's Almond Cake

Ingredients

6 large eggs
150 grams of ground almonds
6 large heaped tablespoons of caster sugar
The zest of one lemon

Instructions

Pre- heat the oven to 180 degrees Celsius
Butter and line a springform cake tin
Separate the egg yolks from the whites
Whisk the egg whites until stiff
Combine the egg yolks with the sugar until pale in colour and then add in the ground almonds and lemon zest
Gently fold in the stiffened egg whites to the mixture
Pour into the pre- prepared tin
Bake at 180 degrees Celsius for 10 mins before reducing the heat to 160
Keep an eye on the cake and reduce further, if need be, to 150/ 140
After 30/ 35 minutes the cake should be ready
Test with a toothpick which should come out clean
Leave to cool before slicing in half
Spread homemade chocolate mousse over one layer and then place the other layer of sponge on top

APPENDIX 2
Kibbutz Cake

You will need 36 petit beurre square biscuits

Cream cheese filling

1 glass of milk
150g butter
1 egg
250g soft white cheese
Vanilla essence

Chocolate cream filling

150g butter
100g sugar
100g halva
¼ glass of milk
3 heaped tablespoons of cocoa powder

Instructions

Dip the biscuits lightly in the milk. Place the biscuits on baking paper in rows of three - you will end up with 3 columns of 6 biscuits. Make the cream cheese by mixing the butter, sugar, egg and vanilla essence together. Use a third of the mixture and spread a layer over the biscuit arrangement. Then place a further 18 biscuits lightly dipped in milk on top of the cream cheese filling. Holding the baking paper on the long side, lift up to make a triangle shape. Hold together firmly, making sure that there are no gaps in the cake. Place the cake in the fridge overnight.

To make the chocolate cream: boil the butter, sugar, halva, milk and cocoa powder together. Once melted, pour over the cake and then let it set in the fridge.

www.ingramcontent.com/pod-product-compliance
Lightning Source LLC
Chambersburg PA
CBHW032104090426
42743CB00007B/225